Transitions
A Biblical Journey of Womanhood
Shayla Hicks

Lincross Publishing
2017

Copyright © 2017 by Shayla Hicks

"Scripture taken from the HOLY BIBLE, NEW INTERNATIONAL VERSION ®. Copyright © 1973, 1978, 1984 by International Bible Society. Used by permission of Zondervan. All rights reserved."

"Scripture taken from The Message. Copyright © 1993, 1994, 1995, 1996, 2000, 2001, 2002. Used by permission of NavPress Publishing Group."

All rights reserved. This book or any portion thereof may not be reproduced or used in any manner whatsoever without the express written permission of the publisher except for the use of brief quotations in a book review or scholarly journal.

First Printing: 2017

ISBN: 978-0-9987566-7-7

Ordering Information:

Special discounts are available on quantity purchases by corporations, associations, educators, and others. For details, Shayla Hicks at contact information below.

U.S. trade bookstores and wholesalers:

Address: P.O. Box 822014, Vicksburg, MS 39182

Email: transitions061@gmail.com

Website: www.shaylahicks.com

Dedication

For Richard: My Love, Leader, and Friend.

Without your dedication and "gentle" nudging, this book would still be

a dream deferred.

Contents

Acknowledgements ix
Foreword x
Preface xiii
Eve: A Wife of Influence 3
Esther: They Did Not Know Who She Was 18
Abigail: The Fool's Wife 26
Proverbs 31 36
The Shunammite Woman: The Well-To-Do Woman .. 53
Michal: The One Who Brings Him Down 64
The Woman with Issues 75
Abishag: The One Who Warms His Bed 87
The Woman Who Has Become Too Comfortable 95
Prayer Warrior 114
Conclusion 131
About the Author 133
How to Contact 134

Acknowledgements

I would first like to thank God, who is the author and finisher of my faith, and the author of this book. To my parents, thank you for my foundation in the faith and your commitment to leading me in the path of righteousness. To my little brothers, thank you for your tenacity to live your dreams, this encourages me daily. Thank you to my family who is my biggest fan club. To my friends who read chapters and encouraged me along the way, I am so grateful for your support. Richard, your love drives me daily. Chloe and Chase, you are my spring board for inspiration because I want to be my best self as an example to you both.

Thank you Kayla Martin for the initial edits of my book; you made my words come alive by putting them in a format that was tangible and real. Lastly, I would like to thank Lincross Publishing for their integrity and dedication to giving this first time author a chance to make her oldest dream come true.

Foreword

When I first encountered my wife, the first thing I noticed was that she was in transition. I could instantly see her love for God and how His hand was on her. I could also see in the spirit that God wanted to do so much more in her life. She was right on the cusp of a new level, and I knew I had to be a part of cultivating it. I also knew that our paths were compatible.

It would have been a different story if I saw her transition as a threat to God's purpose for my life. If that were the case, I would have had to walk away. Instead, I saw that she was rooted in God and that whatever changes she went through, our future would be secure in God.

Through the years that we have been together, she is ever changing into a new woman. Not in the frightening way of becoming someone I do not recognize, but in the powerful way she has handled the shift in the roles she has had to play as my wife, mother of my children, and spiritual leader. I used the word powerful because she has overcome both trial and triumph in her journey and God's strength has taught her to walk in each of the mantles she has been given. It is amazing to see both her successes and her failures.

Most little girls have dreams for their lives. Some imagine their Prince Charming riding in on a white horse to steal their hearts. Others have been conditioned to create a fairytale where they are center stage and get to save themselves. Even little boys rehearse the day that they will find true love and set out to conquer the world, but few ponder the movement, development, or adaptation it requires to bring those yearnings to pass. This process is called Transition, and this is what has been so vividly captured in this book from a biblical viewpoint: the progression of womanhood. Women wear so many hats—daughter, mother, sister, friend, wife, just to name a few. These are all titles that women navigate at different stages of their lives. How often do these ladies go from one function to the next without fully understanding the significance of the process?

Do you have the desire to be the best God has called you to be but need more guidance? Do you know someone who is not completely where they should or want to be in their personal development? Are you a man that knows a woman who is pondering these very questions? If you answered yes to any of these, then do not put down this book.

I became a minister nine years ago, and recently became a Pastor. Throughout that time, I have been asked these very questions in the hopes that I could provide some magical answer. I have heard many compelling and even sad stories from women about heartbreak and personal loss. The truth is that the only answer to be given is from a biblical standpoint.

Shayla has prayed that God will give her these answers to provide to the many women she encounters in ministry. Her heart is heavy with the burdens she sees women carry. We often talk about what God will have her do to be a part of the solution. And through much prayer and divine intervention *Transitions* was written. Just like every other woman in this world, Shayla is constantly evolving. Even in marrying me she was faced with having to segue very quickly from single life to being married, co-parenting a teenage daughter, and becoming the wife of a pastor. She has always used the Bible as her guide in navigating her new life. And now, she wants to teach other women to do the same. In this book, she explores the ability of women to adjust their ministry and their everyday lives to be more far-reaching and effective through the example of the Word of God.

Preface

When I finished this book, my family was right in the middle of starting a new church ministry. Talk about a transition! Although my husband had been a minister for years, he had never been a pastor. I had only been a minister's wife for three years, and that in itself was a transition. The one thing I can say with assurance is that God's grace is sufficient. I began to see that every prior experience had brought me to this point and they had taught me lessons that I could now apply.

I grew up a church girl. My family made a commitment to follow Christ when I was at the tender age of six. I am sure that was a transition for them. My father was on his way to an attorney's office to file for divorce when someone on the street shared with him the message of Christ. He came and got my mom, and they went to church and accepted Christ. With two small children and an infant, they had to make major changes in their lives in order to line up with the Word of God. They lost some friends, and some family members did not understand this "new life" they decided to live. I cannot remember much of my life changing other than instead of listening to Michael Jackson we now listened to Maranatha music. If you have never heard of Maranatha, just search for it on the internet. Trust me, going from Michael Jackson to Maranatha is a major change.

Although my conversion to Christianity at six was not at first momentous, that changed as I became older. Transitioning through adolescence is already a difficult feat, but to do so as an alien (as the Bible refers to Christians due to our stance to be different from the carnal man) is added pressure. I went through those years living what seemed to be a double life. I would try to please God and my friends simultaneously.

When I graduated high school and went to college, I decided to live how I wanted to live. For nearly a year, I rarely went to church. I did everything I did not have an opportunity to do when I was at home. The thing is, there was only so far I could go with God's Spirit on the inside of me. The guilt would overwhelm me. From that point until my early adulthood, I had a hard time transitioning to any phase of life with peace.

Finally, after bumping my head over and over, I recommitted my life to Christ. My challenges did not end, but I found a new way to deal with them: applying the Word of God. I developed a love for the scriptures. The stories in between the soft pages were no longer boring—just the opposite, in fact. The words came to life and began to mirror my day-to-day trials. The Bible became my go-to for every situation.

Truly, there is nothing new under the sun. Every plot twist found on the most popular soap opera can be found in the Bible. Sabotage. Revenge. Adultery. Murder. Redemption. Power couples. Power struggles. If you are suffering from infertility problems, it happened in the Bible. Having trouble in your marriage? There is a reference in the Bible. Is your child acting a fool and ruining your reputation? The Bible covers that, too.

Even before I became a pastor's wife, people would come to me with their problems. I always like to have an example from the Word. I could tell my testimony or my opinion on the matter, but only when I backed up my example with the Word would it make a difference. We overcome by the blood of the lamb and the word of our testimony, but our testimony only has life in the scriptures. Yes, I was able to transition from an unholy union to a godly marriage, as you will find out in this book, but it was not without the stories of biblical heroines like Abigail who was unhappily married and later married a king.

In this book, I want to encourage you to rely on the Bible as you encounter transitions on your journey of womanhood. Yes, we can talk to our sisters, girlfriends, or our coworkers. Sometimes we receive good advice, and other times their wisdom can make the situation even worse. But we can never go wrong with God's examples.

Eve: A Wife of Influence

And the Lord God said, it is not good that man should be alone; I will make a help meet for him.

Genesis 2:18 (KJV)

One of the major transitions of my life has been learning how to be a godly wife. At the beginning of my marriage, I had a major struggle with total submission to my husband. By nature, I am a submissive person who does not normally buck against the system. In most cases, I will go along with the plan to keep the peace. Before I met my husband, I was recovering from a divorce that left me broken and unable to trust easily, especially when it came to men. For six years, I was single, and through trials and circumstance, I built a trusting relationship with God, where I began to consistently rely on the voice of the Holy Spirit to lead me in all things.

Fast forward to marriage and the process of having to relinquish that control to someone else, especially in major life decisions—let me just say, it ain't easy. My husband is a godly man. During our courtship, I appreciated that he was patient to pray things through and not make rash decisions; it was one of the things that attracted me to him.

When I met him, he had just started a job that had been offered to him over a year prior, but he did not take the job until God told him to. It is funny how the thing that I loved while we were courting was the thing that became a source of contention in the early transition of our marriage. I am not the most patient person. I see a vision, and usually, once I have received it I go full speed ahead with a plan of attack.

If I find out on Monday morning that I have to move in a month, by Monday afternoon I have a plan. My husband, also a visionary, has a totally different approach. He may come to me and say, "God showed me this," yet it may be two months later before I even hear about it again. Even with decisions we have to make about our family, he is slow to speak until he knows exactly what God is leading him to do. In the meantime, I am thinking, "Can you at least give me a clue of what God might be saying?"

In this area our lives, we had to learn to balance each other. I had to learn to let him lead by the guidance of the Holy Spirit, and he had to learn that although God gives him the authority to lead, he has to find ways to make me secure with the plan, even in the waiting.

The miraculous thing about my husband coming to this realization was that I did not have to nag him to get to that point. Well, if I am honest, I did start out doing just that. I was quick to tell him that I could hear from God just as well as he, and I made it clear that he needed to include me in the decision-making process.

That didn't help because he became even more silent, and that was frustrating. Then something even more dangerous happened: he began to make decisions to try and make me happy, but they were not necessarily in the plan of God. That just bred an atmosphere of disaster and a prolonging of God's purpose in our marriage.

That strategy did not go over so well. As a matter of fact, God began to chastise me about His order in 1 Corinthians 11:3. "Christ is the head of every man and the head of the woman is man and the head of Christ is God."

As I began to humble myself and pray for God to make a change in me so that I could become a wife who trusts my Husband to lead, God did just that—and he used my husband to help me in that area. Because of his love and tenderness toward me, he began to see that I was not disrespecting his authority. Instead, he recognized that I was dealing with issues of trust that I was holding onto from past hurts in my life. He began to minister to me in those areas with God's grace, and it became easier for me to relinquish the control I was trying to hold onto as a safety net to avoid hurt and disappointment.

The beauty of the whole thing is that because I did not pray to God to change my husband, but rather focused on the places where I needed to be restored, God used someone else to speak to my husband. This is probably one of my favorite examples of God showing His love for me during the early days of my marriage.

I was at the bookstore buying some items, and the cashier asked if I would like to purchase one of the discounted items they had on display at the register. I saw a men's compilation CD series with a few ministers and teachers I recognized by name. I thought my husband would enjoy listening to it on his morning commute to work. I gave it to him, but it sat on the table for at least a week or two.

Around that time, we had a conversation about our individual views on how a husband should lead and how a wife needed to feel secure in his leading. We were not exactly on the same page, but we were closer to agreement than we had ever been on the topic. The following day, he called me on his way home and asked if I had listened to it. I told him I had not, and that it was still sealed when I gave it to him. He began to tell me that one of the messages was speaking to men about laying out a plan before their families and not leaving them in the dark when it came to the decision-making.

I wanted to celebrate, but I stayed composed, and instead of rejoicing in the victory, I began to tell him how God had begun to deal with me about trusting him to make decisions. The Holy Spirit has taught me that when God does a work to bring my husband to a place of change, it is my responsibility to go to a place of even greater submission. Yes, I could have said, "I told you so," and I do, in a sense, every time I tell this story—ha! But my main focus now is to build my husband up with affirmation in the areas where God is increasing him and to let God deal with the areas where he needs to change.

This is not to say that God does not use wives to speak to those tender areas where a man does not allow anyone to enter. God created us to be the help meet taken from the man's body, which means we are a part of him. No one on earth can reach my husband the way I can.

I know when he is weak and tired. I see in his eyes when God gives him a new revelation that he wants to run with but has to keep to himself until God releases him to share it. I see when he tries to cover those hidden places that have been locked up for years. More importantly, I see when he is ready to open up and reveal the most vulnerable parts of himself. The first transition I made as a wife was that I had to learn the power of my influence.

When God placed Adam in the east garden, He gave him the authority to take care of the garden as he saw fit. God made Adam a steward of the garden, which means Adam became an official supervisor of order. In Genesis 2:19, it says that God brought the animals to Adam to see what he would name them. He trusted Adam because he knew that Adam was capable of getting the job done. God deposited into Adam the ability to not only name the animals but the scientific details of species. That is more than ordinary intelligence; that is genius. God Genius. And from that genius, God created woman.

God does not operate on afterthought. He knew on the first day when he said, "Let there be light," that he would create woman. When no suitable helper was found for Adam, God put him in a deep sleep and took one of his ribs. From Adam's rib, He made Eve and brought her to Adam. The Hebrew says that God built Adam a woman, one that was specifically made for him.

I remember when my husband found me. Yes, I said, "found me." He was not on my radar. I knew he existed because I happened to work with his sister, and every day she would talk about her amazing brother. I did not know then that she was on a matchmaking campaign. It was not until we were married that I found out that while she was telling me how wonderful her brother was, she was also telling her brother that she had found the perfect woman for him. We never met or even saw each other during the time I worked at that office, and I am glad about that. The way we met is a much more interesting story that I am sure will be passed down to our children's children.

We met on Tuesday, January 10, 2012, for the first time but didn't speak until the next day. He later told me that he knew then that I would be his wife. I remember that Tuesday morning; my church was on a three day fast, and I remember praying to God while in the shower. I told Him I was ready to receive the man that he wanted me to have. I had previously chosen for myself, and that ended in a devastating divorce. I had some idea of what I wanted in a man, and I had even made a short list. I surrendered my list to God and said, "If this is not what you want for me, then send me what you know I need. I am ready to trust you with this." It had taken me two years after my divorce to even find the courage to date again, and for six years I remained single. When I went out that day, I was running an errand for my aunt, and I had no idea that I was being watched.

The song, "I Won't Turn Back" by William McDowell had recently been released, and I was listening to it on the radio and entering into worship. Worship is the first place where God began to heal me. I am not referring to just singing a song, as I do not think that is what caught my husband's eye. I am speaking of total abandonment of everything you want in exchange for God's plan for your life. When you have that kind of connection with God, it is magnified in everything you do, even in driving and singing in your car. There is a light upon you that cannot go unnoticed.

Several years ago, a prophet came to my church, and I received a prophetic word that I was a fragrance for whatever environment I was in, and that I brought about change and refreshment. I did not know what that meant at the time, but I now know that it means that my connection to God and His Spirit inside of me radiates into the atmosphere to bring light to dark places. It really has nothing to do with me, but everything to do with how I relate to God. I can see the difference around me when I am focused in worship and obedience to God. When I am disciplined in prayer and study of God's Word, things happen in every place my feet tread. When I am spiritually lazy that light dulls and not only do I not have an effect on my environment, but I am also frustrated in my personal life. As women, we have the power to shift the atmosphere.

When Adam was in the Garden, God knew that Adam's life would be incomplete with just the animals for company. I am sure that Eve's presence brought comfort, excitement, and even purpose to him.

A woman can drive a man to conquer more than he would when he is alone because he has a reason to conquer. That does not mean he cannot be successful alone, but having someone that depends on your strength brings focus and propels one to seek direction.

God is so complex, and He does one thing for so many purposes. He knew that one of the benefits of marriage was that the husband would have to draw close to Him in order to lead a family. Any godly man that submits his life to God and then takes a wife can testify that it takes a close relationship with God to keep that woman satisfied. He has to stay on his knees praying to God and asking, "What is it that this woman needs and desires?"

We women are so complex that I am sure it is hard sometimes for a man to understand the language we speak, the emotions we so passionately display, and the things that bring us fulfillment. Only God can help him with this. It is all a continuous cycle of God to Man, Man to Woman, and Woman back to God. It all reverts to a relationship with God. When we connect with God in prayer, we began to understand our purpose, and we develop the spiritual fruit needed to become first a vessel to be used by God, and then suitable for the plan God has given to our husbands for our family.

The biggest mistake we as women make is conforming to fit into what we think God is doing in our husband's life. We do a disservice not only to ourselves but also our husbands. God created both male and female in His image.

In Ephesians 5, God gives specific instructions to husbands and wives individually; therefore, we are created for different purposes, but all in the image of God to perpetuate His plan on the earth. When we see a couple who are walking in sync, it is not because the husband controls the wife by word and deed; it is because they are spiritually in tune with Christ, who leads them both, and thus they can submit to each other. The power of agreement is prevalent in their marriage. Often when I first seek God for what He wants me to contribute to our family, and then when I listen to the vision my husband has received from God, they line up perfectly. We begin to finish each other's sentences.

The Power of Agreement in Marriage

Agreement is a powerful force. Even in the natural, if a house were to be divided, the foundation would be damaged. The entire house may not fall, but it would be weak and in danger of falling apart at any moment. The same is true in a divided marriage. The spouses may live in the same house, but at any moment, their marriage could fall apart and end. The simplest arguments can bring about division. Pride is often the culprit that keeps the two parties from coming together. One person may know that they are dead wrong, but their ego will not let them admit it.

An argument about squeezing the toothpaste from the bottom or letting down the toilet seat becomes a knockdown, drag out fight about why one hates the other's mother. This is Satan's plan to keep unity out of marriage. He knows if the two spouses stand together there is nothing that they cannot accomplish.

Even God confused those attempting to build the Tower of Babel because as he stated in Genesis 11:6, "If as one people speaking the same language they began to do this, then nothing they plan to do will be impossible for them." That is exactly what married couples must do—they must speak the same language and build. The husband is the head of the wife in the same way that Christ is the head of the church. Christ gave His life for the church, and this is what God expects from the husband: to give up his body. This takes us back to the Garden, where God took a part of Adam's side to create the woman. In doing this, God assured that man would always have the responsibility of taking care of woman just as he would himself.

God calls the relation of a husband loving his wife to Christ and the Church—a profound mystery. It has certainly been interpreted in a wide array of ways in passionate debate, often making the word "submission" equivalent to a four-letter word. When we rely on the interpretation of submission from Ephesians, we see that the husband is responsible for watching over the wife as he watches over himself, and the wife is responsible for submitting to her husband as to the Lord.

First, we must be obedient to God, and then submission becomes easier, but if your husband is submitted to God, it will more than likely become a joy.

Regardless of whether or not the husband is submitted to God, wives are commanded to submit. Women are not powerless when it comes to submission. We have the power to choose to whom we will have to submit. This is why the process of dating must be done under the care and instruction of God. God gives us free will in who we marry, but we must remain close to Him in this process so that our eyes and ears will be open to see and hear.

The Woman and The Gift of Perception

I often ask God to give me a revelation of why the serpent chose to go to the woman instead of directly approaching Adam, who was there with the woman. Some may say that the woman was the weaker vessel and easier to deceive, but I would beg to differ. Women by nature are the most perceptive and intuitive beings that God created. We can analyze, dissect, and resolve a situation in a matter of seconds. This is why we can tell our husbands, "Be careful around that woman, she is interested in you," and he will initially say we're overreacting. As time passes, however, he'll admit we were right and that the woman did make a pass at him. That same intuition lets us know when a husband is being unfaithful, when a supposed friend is being shady, or when a loved one is taking advantage of our generosity.

And so, it was with Eve. The serpent, being crafty, knew that Eve would rely on her sense of sight to make a decision. The scripture says that Eve saw that the tree was good for food and pleasing to the eye and that it was desirable for gain.

It is so interesting that God had the same line of vision when He created the earth. Genesis 1:4 says, "God saw that light was good, and he separated the light from the darkness." God invested in women the ability to see a good thing.

I believe this is why a man receives favor in his life when he finds a wife—because a woman has been given the grace to see and attract. Ephesians 4:7-8 reveals that God has apportioned each one a measure of grace and certain gifts to men. Psalm 68 is the complimentary text for this scripture that says God gives gifts even to the rebellious. Even though Eve had a seed of rebellion in her heart, she still had the gift to see. The rebellion is what caused her to sin. Women value the things in which they can see potential. It can be as minute as seeing a pair of shoes in the store that has potential to compliment that outfit we have in our closet or as serious as seeing a man who has the potential to be great with just a bit of encouragement. This trait can be used as a positive or a negative depending on whether we are operating in the flesh or the spirit.

We can reference several examples of women in the Bible who, being led by God, used their influence to turn around a damaged situation. Abigail, the wife of Nabal, a wealthy but prideful man, was obviously a woman of influence in her home. It was she who the servants came to when her husband had set himself up to die by angering David. She gathered up food and set out on her donkey to rectify a dangerous situation her husband had created.

Esther was able to save her people because of the influence she had with her husband. Naomi was able to overcome her bitter emotions and coach her daughter-in-law to marry into the lineage of Christ. Mary, the mother of Jesus, showed strength in a situation that could have been seen as a Jerry Springer moment with her unexplainable pregnancy and birth of the Savior of the World.

Just as we have positive examples from the Bible of people who used their influence for good, we also have examples that teach us how not to use our influence. Delilah preyed on the weakness of Samson and destroyed not only him but an entire city. Jezebel tried to rule over her husband, and she ended up dead in a pile of vomit. Bathsheba gave into the lust of David, and her life became a scandal. Michal, the wife of David, despised her husband and that scorn produced bitterness in her heart. Whether or not you see yourself or someone you know in the heroines of the Bible, I pray this book helps you to see what God sees: A woman of God in transition.

Esther:

They Did Not Know Who She Was

But Esther had kept secret her family background and nationality just as Mordecai had told her to do, for she continued to follow Mordecai's instructions as she had done when he was bringing her up.
Esther 2:20 (NIV)

There is a four-letter word that has plagued me for many years, and I am certain that it is a crutch to you as well. That word is "fear." Fear of not having what it takes to accomplish my goals and dreams has been the main source of stagnation in my God-aligned purpose. I am not even certain of the source of this terror. Certainly, I was trained in the church as a child and taught Philippians 4:17. It was drilled into me by my parents. I won the candy for reciting it in children's church, and I confessed it in those moments when my plan was to divide and conquer. On the surface, I was proclaiming it, but I did not have the faith and belief to really own the power behind God's promise in that scripture.

This is not to say I have not accomplished great things or had success in my life, but there is always that door of exceeding abundance that God is waiting to take me through that has a screen door blocking it. A screen door is used for minimal protection; it blocks the outside elements but still allows you to see and enjoy what is on the other side of the door. In my case, the screen door was a hindrance. I could see all the opportunities I wanted to enjoy, but the door was preventing me from getting to them.

Even in the writing of this book, it took encouragement and reminders from others that God gave me a gift to share with the world. As I think on their encouragement, I reflect on countless times that people have called on me to help write recommendation letters, professional letters, resumes, and even college essays.

According to those requesting parties, I just know how to convey what they are trying to say. Even with all the encouragement, I believe the driving force to finally moving forward with this manuscript was the need for it among my sisters in Christ.

As we know from Romans 8:19, creation is waiting for what we have in order for it to be delivered from bondage. What God inspires me to say in this book will help some woman who is transitioning in her life to overcome the obstacles before her. This is the place at which we as women of God have to arrive—the place of unapologetic purpose. We have to put down fear, selfishness, and false humility and begin to soar in the areas where God has given us authority. We are fearfully and wonderfully made, and God knows exactly who we are and what He created us to accomplish. When I began to realize how foolish it is for me to say to my manufacturer, God, "Oh, I know you created me to perform this way, but I have a malfunction," everything began to change. The myth I want to dispel in this chapter is that we as women have malfunctioned in life, or that because of past mistakes we are damaged goods.

God says, "Not so," and God doesn't lie!

In the many times I have heard the story of Esther, not much was said about her being an orphan. I have heard how she was chosen from many as Queen because she won the favor of her husband, the King. Esther is revered for risking her life for her people's freedom, but what about the little orphan girl taken in by her cousin?

I could ask this same question regarding many women today, particularly in the Kingdom of God. People talk about how great Sister Sally sings or how Sister Sue organized that program so well, but no one knows that the reason her voice is filled with raw emotion when she sings is because she is singing about the pain of the rape she experienced when she was a little girl. No one has translated Sister Sue's overcompensation in every area of her life as desperation to be better than the rough part of town from which she came.

It's Time to Stop Hiding

Some women are like Esther. They keep their family background or those things which make them different a secret because someone told them, "You are from the wrong side of the tracks, so just fake it till you make it." Like Esther, they are just following the instructions of their kinfolk. Others do not need anyone to discourage them, as they have that market cornered themselves. That was me. After my divorce, all I heard in my head was, "You are damaged goods."

I believed that no Christian man would want to marry me because of the stigma of divorce. We all know how unforgiving some "church" men can be. They have taken loving their wife like Christ loves the church to the next level. They, too, are looking for a bride without spot or wrinkle—literally! The insecurity I felt during this time was so palpable that I just decided to keep my head down and not even worry about dating.

The sad part about me taking this stance was that I was not the initiator of wrongdoing in my marriage or even in the action of divorce. I took on someone else's guilt and shame when Christ had nailed mine to the cross. Women are receivers, and so many times we just accept whatever is handed to us, whether it is a minimal station in life or someone's leftovers.

As your sister in Christ, I am asking you to do just one thing: Stop! Stop hiding from who you are or where you come from and realize you are worthy because you are adopted. We have a father who adopted us as His Beloved and our Father owns it all; therefore, we have the right to subdue any area of life we want. I get chills just thinking about it as I write. How many missed opportunities have passed me by, when all I had to do was just walk through the door and say, "My Father said you would be expecting me"?

It is important not to let your current or past station in life hinder where you are going. What if Esther had decided that because she was a Jew, she was not good enough for the King? Not only would she have not fulfilled her destiny of becoming a queen, but the Jews, God's chosen people, would have been destroyed. You are God's chosen, and your destiny is not just for your benefit. What you have is good enough for any circle.

Take the girl without any formal education that attracts that CEO. People around cannot understand how she landed a guy like that—after all, what do they have in common?

It is the Pretty Woman movie in real life. I always desired for there to be a sequel to that movie so that we could see how Julia Roberts's character navigated the world of the rich and famous. It is not what the successful man and the girl next door have in common but what she has that he needs and is attracted to—strength, common sense and wisdom. There are many sharks in corporate America, and a girl from the streets is not easily intimidated or frazzled. She knows how to build from nothing and start over if there is a need. A more privileged girl may not be able to handle her husband coming home and saying, "We lost it all, and we have to rebuild." She may not be apt at eating Top Ramen when all she is used to is prime rib. Instead of focusing on what was missing from your past, why not reflect on what it took for you to overcome and use those experiences to propel you to the next level?

Although I wanted to take the time to focus on Esther overcoming the obstacle of being an orphan, I do not want to minimize the importance of her preparation for royalty status. I have often heard that success is preparation meeting opportunity. When your time comes to walk through an open door, you do not want to say, "I need a minute."

The truth is you will not get that minute; instead, the door will be closed to you and opened to another person. It is easy for a dreamer to let their imagination run on forever, but at some point, you must move forward in the creative process and take steps to turn that dream into reality.

It may impress some people that Esther and the other women vying for the position of Queen completed twelve months of beauty treatments, but what stands out to me is that Esther found favor with Hegai, the King, and everyone who saw her. She found favor both with the person that could put her in the position to be chosen and with the one doing the choosing. We must find favor with the One who has access to everything we need, and that is God. His favor will open doors that no man can shut. It does not matter who knows us or what they know about us—if God chooses us, our success is guaranteed.

Abigail: The Fool's Wife

The Lord Your God will certainly make a lasting dynasty for my Lord's battles, and no wrongdoing will be found in you as long as you live.
1 Samuel 25:28 (NIV)

All the signs were there from the beginning ; I just ignored them. We were college sweethearts, so I thought that since we loved each other, it was the right time to get married. Never mind the infidelities or that sinking feeling I felt on the day we were married. I thought it was just normal to have nerves on the day you say, "I do." He was a good guy with a big heart, and we were best friends. We could talk about anything or nothing at all. He made a confession of faith before we were married and received the gift of tongues, so he seemed to be prepared to serve God whole-heartedly.

I guess it is important to backtrack and explain that when we initially met in college and began dating, I was in a backslidden state, and though he was a Christian, he did not have any visible fruit. Our core moral values were the same, such as loving your neighbor and believing that God is the source of all good things. Past that point, things were definitely in the gray area. Since I was not in fellowship with God, I overlooked all his wrongdoing that did not line up with the Word of God because, if I confronted his sin, I would have to evaluate my own.

It was just safe to ignore his transgressions along with mine. I pushed to the back of my mind the fact that if God was merciful to let me live through my sin phase, I would one day reconcile my faith and then have to confront the fact that we were unequally yoked.

Fast forward two years to when we decided to get married, and he received the gift of the Holy Spirit.

Everything seemed to change, and I thought I had dodged a bullet. We would pray together. I would wake in the middle of the night to him praying over me, and we began to line up our lives with the Word of God. He was immediately questioned by friends and family about "this new lifestyle he was trying to live" and "why he had to make all these changes just to be with me." It was hard for him, and I can now understand why. My spiritual walk had been cultivated since I was six years old, so even though there was a period that I was out of fellowship with God once I repented it was like riding a bike. For him, adjusting to the way I served God was like learning to fly a plane, and since he was not a certified pilot, no one in his life wanted to fly with him. They were only used to him driving a car. I could not see it this way at that time because I was too concerned about my happily ever after.

Unfortunately, my fairy tale quickly turned into a nightmare. It all started when he went on a business trip and came back different. Even to this very day, I cannot say exactly what happened while he was away. I have my theories, but nothing was proven. I just know we were no longer in sync. He was now questioning whether he authentically decided to make the changes in his life by his own choice or by my ultimatum. I had told him before we married that I had made a decision to serve God and that the man I married had to also live a righteous life. I am not sure what his motivation was at the time he asked me to marry him, but I have to be honest about mine.

Although I did have a desire to marry a Christian man, I also did not want to live in sin any longer. The two of us had fornicated in college, and now that I had made a recommitment to God I did not want to fall back into sin. This is not the right motivation for marriage. God did not create marriage as a way of escape; he created marriage as a means to illustrate His glory through unconditional love and covenant. My impure intentions were quickly revealed when we did not even make it through the engagement without falling back into sin. This is how the enemy works—he convinces you that you can dictate your own future rather than rely on God's plan.

Our marriage was a constant three years of fighting, tolerance, and sometimes just plain hell. I would wake up before the sun came up to pray and he would tell me I was too loud. I would go to church on Sundays, but when I returned home, we would argue. If he made me mad enough, I would cuss him out, and later feel condemned and defeated. I think we both were sorry about how we were making the other feel. By the end of our last year together, I think both of us were in a depression and ready for it to be over. He knew that because of my faith, I did not believe in divorce except for infidelity, so he began to tell me he was unfaithful—which was probably true, but I know the only reason he told me was so I could divorce him. That was the worst feeling in the world, knowing that he wanted to be rid of me so badly that he was willing to expose himself as a means to an end.

Looking back now with clarity, I believe that he was not only concerned about his well-being, but he was also trying to give me an out.

He knew that we would probably never be on the same page when it came to how we interpreted our faith and that things would not get better. The sad part is that God's hand could have redirected the course of our marriage had we been on one accord, but because we could not come to an agreement, our marriage ended. Thankfully, God turned what the devil meant for evil into something for my good.

Living Unequally Yoked

The biblical account of David, Nabal, and Abigail, found in 1 Samuel 25, illustrates the life of a woman who knew how to navigate being married to an unbeliever. Nabal, Abigail's husband, was a wealthy man who owned quite a bit of property. The Bible says he was mean and surly in his dealings. This is obviously not the character of a godly man. Not only was Nabal wicked, but he also lived up to his name—he was foolish.

Abigail was the opposite of her husband, as the Bible describes her as intelligent and beautiful. It is hard not to wonder how this woman who seemingly had a good head on her shoulders ended up with an imprudent and prideful man. Was he a different person when she met him? Did the circumstances of life cause him to become bitter and hateful? Maybe Abigail married him for money. She would not be the first woman in history to marry for money and later have to pay in tears for her choice. Many women seek to marry accomplished men without first counting up the cost.

Success sometimes is associated with long working hours and an egotistic behavior. The pain of loneliness will soon outweigh status and access to material possessions. Do not misunderstand me, a woman is not amiss in wanting to be connected to a man of achievement or means, but if he is not connected to God, then therein lies the issue. Also, a woman must examine her motives and her heart if her measuring stick for compatibility is rooted in what a man can offer her financially. A woman's goal should be to align herself with a man of purpose, and one whose purpose complements her own. A purpose-driven marriage breeds success and access without distress. It is important for a woman to ask God to really show her the man she is courting for marriage.

While we were dating, I had to inquire of God to open my eyes to the uncovered areas of my now husband's life. God answered me, and some of the things I saw should have frightened me, but because I knew he was my husband, I was not afraid. Instead, I drew closer to God to inquire if the man I was dating was willing to face his issues. Once God let me know that he was ready to be healed of his hurts, I asked for insight on how to minister to those areas once we were married. This is the key. You have to know God is telling you that this is the person you should marry and you must allow God to complete the work. You are just a vessel he will use to minister to that man's wounds. A man at his most vulnerable state is the same as clay in a potter's hand. He can be shaped into something beautiful with the right technique, or the outcome can become a total mess if not carefully handled.

Marriage is a mirror, so when I look into my husband's eyes, I see myself. If I see hurt in his eyes, I know it is a reflection of me, because we are now one and I have to go to God in prayer on behalf of us both.

The problem that Abigail faced is the same as many women today. In the text, the servant who warned her of Nabal's behavior toward David made a powerful statement. He told Abigail that Nabal was such a wicked man that no one could talk to him. If a man cannot or will not take instruction from anyone, then he is a danger to himself and all those to whom he is connected. Most men are slow to accept advice or ask for help. That is why a man will drive around lost for hours before he asks for directions. Even given his pride, there should be at least one person on earth from whom he will accept instruction.

That is a warning sign for women who are courting. If a man does not have someone he is accountable to, that will be a problem in the relationship. Yes, he should be accountable to God, but he should also be accountable to someone in the flesh. Proverbs 27:17 says, "Iron sharpens iron; so, a man sharpens his friend's countenance." For some men, once they are married, their wife becomes their main accountability partner, though there are still things regarding manhood to which she will not be able to speak. Apparently, Abigail did not have this type of relationship with her husband, because she did not talk to him about the issue with David to see if she could reason with him.

Along with my questions of how Nabal and Abigail came to be, I marvel at the possibility that the incident with David was not Abigail's first encounter during which she had to apologize for Nabal's irreverent behavior. After all, even the servants knew to run and report how "her man" had treated King David.

This is evidence of a pattern of reckless conduct and also insecurity on the part of Nabal. Rather than accept the opportunity to bring honor to the man of God, he chose to mock him and question his position.

Usually, when a man challenges another man's identity, it is a result of a lack of self-confidence. It is to be expected that if Nabal exhibited discourteous manners with David that Abigail was also on the receiving end of his arrogance. She was obviously skilled in coming to his defense when he was rash, for she reacted quickly even when the servants told her to think it over. This is definitely a characteristic of a mistreated woman: quick to protect. Always ready with an excuse to cover for her man. I can imagine that Abigail was embarrassed, and she surely was angry that her husband had once again placed her in a tumultuous circumstance. Her eagerness to call him out to David as wicked and foolish is proof of her fury. Even in her annoyance, she still tried to right his wrong because she knew that he had brought death to their door.

The Bible states that when a man finds a wife, he finds a good thing and obtains favor from God. In some cases, that favor is taken for granted and therefore; undeserved. However, the scripture did not put any conditions on receiving this favor, so even when a man is not a good husband, he still collects the reward. My belief is that the man still obtains favor because a woman's love is often without merit. Even when mistreated, a good woman will deny her needs to be devoted to her husband. In the case of a Christian woman married to an unsaved man, it is often her prayers that are the root of his success and his salvation.

It is unfortunate that so many men are comparable to Nabal in that they sabotage everything their wives do to establish blessings in their home with their carnality. However, it is unfair to place blame on just the man. In cases where a woman knowingly marries an unbeliever, she should expect there to be some division in the home. This is the reason why it is commanded that believers not be unequally yoked with unbelievers. God, in His wisdom, attempts to keep us out of the pitfalls of carnal ideologies.

2 Corinthians plainly states that the believer and unbeliever have nothing in common. Eventually, the believer may win over her unsaved husband, but it will not happen overnight in most cases. The one thing that is assured is that if the saved woman remains faithful to God even in the midst of her despondent marriage, God will either change her husband's heart, deliver her from the marriage as he did Abigail, or give her the strength to endure until the end.

Proverbs 31

Do not spend your strength on women,
your vigor on those who ruin kings.
Proverbs 31:3 NIV

Proverbs 31 begins with words of wisdom spoken to King Lemuel by his mother, warning him not to be yoked with the type of woman who would ruin kings. Most Christian women have aspired to be as resourceful as the wife of noble character, but they rarely dwell on the beginning of the text which is a warning of what not to do. There are many examples of virtuous heroines in the Bible, but there are also examples of the variety of women to which the king's mother was referring. Delilah is an example of a woman who preys on the weaknesses of men. We all have seen this type of woman. She knows she has no real interest in the man but is using him for material gain or her and her friends' amusement.

Many women played this game in college. I can recall nights when I would sit in the dorm with friends, and someone would call that weak guy who would buy dinner for us all. We would laugh and make fun of the "sucker" who is always willing to do whatever for attention. Just as it was with Delilah, this can be a dangerous game to play. When Delilah initially tried to find the secret to Samson's strength, he continuously fooled her into thinking she had the upper hand when, in fact, he was lying to her.

In the same manner, the joke is also on college girls who use men for folly. Just as she and her friends are finding merriment in his actions, he is doing the same with his friends. He is spinning tales of how he can get this particular girl to prostitute herself for possessions. There are some men who will not stop at fictitious accounts of conquest.

They actually expect a return on their investment, be it sex or ownership and may become violent if they are unable to collect.

The big girl version of this game is somewhat similar, but the difference is that grown women are using men for more than just merriment or for the sake of a new outfit. For some women, survival is the name of the game. Rather than rely on God as her source, that single mother sleeps with a male benefactor because she needs money, even though she has no interest in a relationship. She convinces herself that it is for her children's sake. One may ask how her actions hurt the man rather than herself—the helpless mother with children.

After all, he has to realize that the end of all their sessions requires him to pay up to play. The reality is that though she is not alone in blame, she is assisting in ruining his potential. If men always have women who are willing to accept only the bare minimum of what they can offer, they will never reach their true level of kingship. Not to mention that since she is not truly interested in him, she is reducing the value of another woman's king. Due to the experience he has had with her, he will see all women as liabilities rather than assets because, in his experience, they only take from him.

The Delilah Factor

There is a class of women who seek out men of power for more than the ability to subsist. They want to conquer. There is no historical account of Delilah and Samson's relationship before Delilah was approached by the rulers of the Philistines. The text only states that Samson was in love with Delilah, but it does not say that she was in love with him.

Samson was a powerful judge, but he had something in common with most powerful men—he was weak to the prowess of the woman he loved. His first wife, with her tears, moved him to explain the riddle that no one could figure out. She betrayed him by giving the answer to her people, but the Spirit of the Lord enabled him to overcome in that situation. Instead of learning his lesson, however, Samson fell for the same trick with Delilah, and he was ultimately destroyed by her deceit. Perhaps Delilah thought that she would make a name for herself as the woman who brought down the powerful Samson.

Today there are women who are just as addicted to the power they can get from being with a well-known man. Power is seductive because it is connected to purpose. When someone is operating in their God-given calling, they are illuminated in the eyes of all who see them. There is a natural attraction to light, and this is why women are drawn to powerful men, in both the natural and spiritual world. It does not matter to them if that man is someone's husband.

Usually, what is done in the dark is brought to light, and that man loses everything he has worked for while the woman is on to the next unsuspecting victim. It must be exhausting to play games in order to maintain a certain lifestyle. I always wonder what would happen if women in the game decided to use their prowess to start a business or head up a company. The same skills of negotiating and thinking on your feet used to shake down some man could be used in the boardroom.

The need for instant gratification often outweighs the benefit of enjoying the fruit of hard work, though. Even with Delilah, she let the promise of quick money blind her from seeing with whom she was in a relationship. Rather than deceiving Samson, she could have recognized that he was a powerful man connected to a powerful God. Why did it not dawn on her that if the rulers were willing to pay that kind of money to destroy Samson, she could invest a little time and energy in the relationship to get a better return?

The same goes for women who prostitute themselves for money, clothes, and bags. They could invest in a relationship with Christ who is the source from which all good things flow. You may be single, but you have a husband: God is your husband. I love the text in Isaiah 54 where God assured Israel that He was their husband and that He would have compassion on them, even though for a while He abandoned them out of anger at their disobedience. God feels the same way about His people today. He is concerned about you as a single woman, even when you were not concerned about His will for your life.

When you believed that you needed a sponsor instead of His hand, God was there waiting patiently for you. You may have gone through hard times while you were in sin because God is a just God, but more importantly, He forgives quickly, and He restores what was once lost.

Becoming A Noble Woman

It is never too late to make a change from a woman who ruins kings to one who is of noble character. The difference between the two is that the latter brings her husband "good and not harm all the days of his life," as mentioned in Proverbs 31:12. Normally, when I would read Proverbs 31, I would zero in on how well the wife's house was kept or how early in the morning she had to get up to accomplish all her tasks. Relief set in when I realized that in order to be the best wife I could be, I only needed to live up to the standards of my home.

This passage is often misinterpreted to mean if we do not check off every attribute of the Proverbs 31 woman then we have failed as wives. That is just not the truth. I can honestly say that domestication hasn't always been my area of expertise. The level of multi-tasking it requires to keep a home often escapes me. I am a visionary in my own right, so I can see things accomplished in my head, but the execution leaves something to be desired. My attention span is just too short. Go figure that my husband loves his home clean and he loves to eat. He not only loves to eat, but his children love to eat. I should not have been surprised when my newborn was delivered into the world with a healthy appetite.

As a single woman, I was used to eating a sandwich and a bowl of cereal if I did not feel like cooking. That was no longer an option, so I began to ask the Holy Spirit to help me to be a homemaker or house manager.

This is exactly what the Proverbs 31 woman did—she managed her home. There is nothing like a woman with a plan. One line that really stands out in chapter 31 of Proverbs is, "Her husband has full confidence in her and lacks nothing of value." I decided to dig into this statement and examine myself to see whether my husband could have full confidence in me. First, I had to define what it means to a man to have confidence in his wife. I went directly to the source and asked my husband. His interpretation was that a man with confidence in his wife does not have to micromanage her day; he trusts her to do the right things concerning the family.

His explanation took me to something my father stands by as rule of leadership. He always told me that strong leaders appoint people they know can handle the task and then stay out of their way because they have faith that they will accomplish the mission. You see, a visionary does not have time to stick around and iron out the details, and neither does a successful husband.

For a husband, he needs to trust that his wife is not idle in the home, or that she is not mismanaging the finances because she wants a new outfit and shoes. It only takes a man one or two experiences to form an opinion concerning what type of woman he has. Some men are watching closely during the courtship for signs of what is to come when he asks for that woman's hand in marriage. He may do a visual inspection of your home when he comes to pick you up for a date. It is likely that if your home is untidy as a single person, then he can expect that you are not going to clean his house. If every time he speaks with you, you are at the mall shopping, then you better believe he is weighing the question of whether he can afford you.

The Proverbs 31 woman was also a visionary, so she, too, left some of the details to someone else. She had help in the form of maidservants; therefore, we as women should not be afraid to ask for and accept help. When I had my baby, I turned into some type of superwoman. I felt the only way to have things done the way I wanted them was to do them myself. That lasted only a couple of months. After I was sleep-deprived and broken down, I quickly called in the forces.

There are still days when it's close to time for me to pick up my teenager from school, which is around the time my husband gets off work, and I ask myself, "Where did the time go?" I am often trying to finish dinner while my baby is crying, and when I think I am not going to get all that I want accomplished, I simply say, "God help me." Immediately, either my phone rings or there is a knock on the door from my mom coming to spend time with my daughter. She'll either scoop her up so I can finish my tasks, or help me clean or finish dinner. When you call on God, He will come to your aid. Not only is God there for you, but there are people in your corner who want to assist you.

Everyone cannot afford a maid or a nanny, but maybe you have a single friend or family member who wants to serve. The benefit is that you are receiving help, but they are also gaining companionship.

They may need to help you as much as you need to be helped. Not only are they lending a helping hand, but they are planting seeds for their future family, not to mention getting much-needed practice in the area of domestication.

It helps when you are confident in your ability as a wife. Starting out in my marriage, I always asked my husband's opinion on everything. I wanted everything to be perfect for him, so I felt the best way to do that was to get his approval on everything. If a man feels he has to babysit you in every little task, then he will not have confidence in your ability to run the house. There are areas where you will need to come together and agree, but this is not likely in small decisions such as what to cook for dinner or what color sheets to put on the bed. The thing is, most women already have their mind made up anyway, they just want their husbands to cosign. When he does not give you the answer you were seeking—which will be often—then you'll be disappointed or do your own thing anyway. Then your husband will get upset because he believes you do not trust his judgment when you could have just made the first call and kept dissension out of your marriage. This is a running joke with my husband and I. I ask him which dress, shoes, or earrings he likes and then go with the opposite of whatever he picks.

At the moment, he gets upset and asks me why I bothered to ask him, but later we laugh about it. The truth is, I was dressing myself when he met me, and I obviously did a good job because he was attracted enough to pursue.

In the Proverbs 31, I do not see anywhere that the husband was present in the wife's decision making concerning the home. Now, do not get me wrong, this is not to say that the husband cannot and should not be involved with the tasks of the home. In today's society, it is necessary in some cases for everyone to pull their weight around the house. I can imagine that since the Proverbs 31 woman's husband was working in the city gates, they came together to decide they needed servants. The husband in this text let his wife run the house how she saw fit, and because she ran it in excellence, he was good with whatever she decided.

I think it is important to point out that the wife of noble character, as the Proverbs 31 is sometimes referred to, was what we today call a go-getter. She worked as what seems to be a real estate agent, she gardened to provide food for her family, she was good at negotiating and trading, she was a giver to the poor, and she was prepared for every circumstance that her family faced. It benefits every godly woman to break each of these positions down in their biblical perspective. Verse 14 says that she was "like the merchant ships," which means she searched for the best deals. Hello, couponers! One of my best friends has mastered the art of the stockpile. We had my baby shower at her home and when my husband saw her laundry cabinets full of detergent he was like, "Whoa!" Instead of getting jealous, I asked for help. She was able to share her tips, and now I have learned how to save money.

The scripture says that the woman brought her food from afar, which means that sometimes she possibly traveled for the best deals, or maybe she just stepped outside of herself and asked for help from others whom she trusted. Some of my favorite times as a young lady were traveling on the church's back-to-school shopping trip. The women of the congregation were informed in advance so that we could save, and we were able to find some amazing deals. Form a group of women where at least one person is financially savvy and make plans to take monthly grocery shopping trips to the bulk retailers or annual school shopping trips. We work better when we work together.

Another characteristic of this exemplary wife is that she was an early riser. I did not truly learn the benefit of this until I became pregnant. Due to insomnia, I found myself up at early morning hours, and I discovered a whole new realm called *peace*. There is something about that uninterrupted pre-dawn time to meditate in prayer and scripture, de-clutter the mind, and get things done. This is the one time that operating in darkness is a good thing. You are awake with the watchmen on the wall, and if you join with them in prayer, God will move on behalf of your family.

The Watchmen I am referring to are found in Isaiah 62. In this chapter, God is explaining how He delights in Jerusalem as a bride, and how He has planted heavenly beings to make petitions day and night for His bride.

The scripture says that the beings give God no peace until He does what He says. This chapter and the one preceding it speaks of God's favor for His people. It is important to note that prayer was still present even in the time of favor; as a matter of fact, it was the driving force. The same is true for us. God still wants to disburse favor on our families, but we as women must stand as the watchmen to pray and see. There goes that word again: *see*. Women who attune their lives to constant communication with God will be warned of Satan's strategies against their husbands and children.

In order to be operational in each area of her day, the Proverbs wife had to have energy. Verse 17 says she worked vigorously and she had strong arms. This means she had to have some sort of exercise regimen. I know you are asking, "When did she find *time* to exercise?", because the struggle is real. I have a gym membership that I rarely use. By the time I clean, cook, take care of all my children's needs and end the night taking care of my husband's needs, I am too tired to sleep, and a workout is out of the question. I have learned that fitness does not have to occur at a facility. I love to dance so putting on some music and moving purposely to get my heart rate up counts as physical exertion. Often you can check off more than one box on your to-do list. Maybe you have an unattended lawn or garden. That is a form of exercise. Mopping the floors in your home is a great arm workout if you use some type of bodily form when doing so. If you have stairs in your home and need to take more than one item up the stairs, do so one item at a time.

Including your husband and your children in your exercise will not only keep you accountable but will also create opportunities for family bonding. The biggest obstacle to getting over is the start up, and there is only one answer to get through the course: just do it. Whenever I am feeling lazy, I give myself a motivational talk, and I look for inspiration. It helps me to look at someone who I think has an attractive body, and that motivates me to put down the chips and chocolate and get moving.

Being healthy is important, not only for looking "snatched" but also because we have a purpose to fulfill. How sad would it be to get to heaven and hear God say, "I had more work for you to accomplish, but your health prevented you from completing my vision for your life?" Lack of energy will become a stumbling block to getting to your next level. When I am sick, or even just tired, all I want to do is take a nap. Most of the time, exhaustion is an issue of our flesh needing to be disciplined with exercise and diet management. The best way to put the flesh under subjection is with scripture. The Bible tells us that man cannot live by bread only but by the Word of God. By fasting, praying, and meditating on scripture, one can begin to train their mind to develop a life of habit, which translates in every area of life.

I know you might be thinking, "I get tired and sleepy when I try to read scripture." This is because you have not made a connection with the Bible as your source of strength. You must continuously meditate on the Word and get an understanding, and then studying it will become a lifestyle, and the Word will rejuvenate you.

What happens is that our flesh gives in to overindulgence, which is a sin. Often, sin causes sluggishness. It is a chain reaction. First, one partakes of sin, whether it is the sin of gluttony or gross sin. Next, he falls into condemnation, which opens the door for depression and illness. When a person is sick and depressed, they rarely want to get out of bed, so exercise and taking care of the tasks of the day are not likely to be accomplished. As sin is eliminated from one's life, so is idleness.

If there was one thing the wife of noble character was not, it was idle. Preparation was her modus operandi. She prepared in advanced so that she would not have to worry about the future. I am sure her husband was never in the shower asking for soap, and she had to run out to the store to get some. Verse 25 says she could laugh at the days to come, which means she was not worried about what was to come because she thought ahead and was organized. Although she probably was a woman of means due to her husband's position among the elders, she still found ways to make money herself. She was that woman that other women watch to see what she and her family are wearing. She and her family were clothed in scarlet and fine purple and linen, which was expensive material. She made bed coverings for their beds and their clothes as well. I know that sewing is not a skill that most women today possess—God knows I do not—but being thrifty with money is an easily obtained talent. I have worn clothes from every price point. It is not about how much it costs, but how you wear it.

I remember when we had to wear camouflage to church for a themed event, and my husband saw a $3.00 top at the dollar store when he went to get household supplies. He said he bought it because he knew I could probably make it work, and I did. I put on a pair of pearls with it—you had to see it, but trust me, it worked—and made it Hollywood fabulous. He is used to me mixing and matching items and coming up with different outfits. When people saw me in my dollar store top, they had no clue where I got it from or how much it cost. The key is not to wait until you absolutely have to have something, but to plan ahead; you are likely to get a great deal.

It is important to remember that how you present yourself and even your children represents not only you but also your husband. A woman married to a respectable man won't go grocery shopping with rollers or a head wrap. If your children are dirty and unkempt every time they are in public, that is a reflection of how the husband provides for his family. Just look at two of the most popular presidents, John F. Kennedy and Barack Obama, and look at how much emphasis was placed on the wardrobe of their wife and children. The day after President Obama's inauguration, I cannot tell you how many women were talking about Michelle Obama's hair, her coat, her shoes, and even her gloves. Within hours J. Crew sold out of the items that Sasha and Malia wore. Perception attracts attention, and substance is the attribute that retains it. We need to pay attention to how we present ourselves not only to the world but to our husbands.

We are often so focused on making sure that a man sees us for more than just our looks that we forget that men are visual. When I was dating my husband, I took great care in how I looked for each date. I did not have a stack of money, but I took the time to do things like painting my nails, and I made sure I looked and smelled good. I would start pampering myself hours before our date. Once we were married and I became comfortable, I begin to not put as much effort into how I looked. Little by little I began to slack off in my appearance until one day; my husband told me he missed his girlfriend. He told me that each time he waited with bated breath to see how I would look when I came to the door. I had to begin to pay more attention to my appearance as his wife. Don't get me wrong, when we would go out in public I always represented him well, but at home, I would be lax. He was not asking me to wear a full face of makeup and heels at home, but a neat ponytail and a little lip gloss go a long way.

Guard Your Home

There are culprits other than sin that come to steal our strength and productivity, such as negative environments and people. As wives, we must watch over the atmosphere of our home. We cannot allow our family, friends, or associates to cause strife or confusion, or just plain meddle in our affairs concerning our husband and children. Everyone has advice on how you should raise your children or how you should relate to your spouse, but many times their advice causes more of a disturbance, especially if it is not based on the Word of God. When we are married, we become one with our husbands, and together we are to make decisions concerning our family.

The Shunammite Woman:
The Well-To-Do Woman

Do not be anxious about anything, but in every situation, by prayer and petition, with thanksgiving, present your requests to God. 7 And the peace of God, which transcends all understanding, will guard your hearts and your minds in Christ Jesus.
Philippians 4:6-7 (NIV)

There is nothing worse than making an assumption of who a person is based on visual perception. Many women have been fooled into thinking that they want another woman's perfect life based on an expensive shoe or bag, especially in this age of social media. A well-lit snapshot can make it easy to lust after someone else's life. The problem is that there is no certainty that there is a perfect life on the other side of that optic.

Ask any broke woman what money means to her, and she would probably say it is the answer to all her problems. Ask a rich woman the same question, and she will probably say the opposite—that money is the cause of some or most of her problems. The Shunammite woman in 2 Kings 4 had a problem that her money could not solve. The text says that the woman was married and well-to-do. She had so much money that she just decided one day to remodel her home for Elisha.

If that does not sound like a life worth coveting, I do not know what does. Most of us have to plan and save just to redecorate, and she decides to build and furnish a room for an occasional guest! Because of the Shunem woman's generosity, Elisha asked his servant what could be done to repay her. When asked what it was she needed or wanted; she responded that she was secure and satisfied with her family. I believe that her response has a two-fold interpretation for how we as women should live.

Some women have this same response when opportunity knocks at their door, but it is not because they are satisfied, but rather because they have a fear of the unknown. I thought it was interesting in the text that when the woman came to Elisha, she stood at the door—an open door. Many women have an open door that they are too afraid to walk through because they have convinced themselves that they should be satisfied with their current portion. We do not want to seem ungrateful or be a bother to anyone because we already have what most consider a good life. Deep inside, however, we know we want more in life, but we settle. The problem is that God did not create us to settle. He created us to subdue and rule.

The other interpretation of the Shunamite woman's answer is that she could have been in a state of contentment. When we are content in our current season, that is when God begins to stretch us for more. Some women are never satisfied. Their husband could build their dream house, furnish it, put a car in the garage and pay someone to clean it, and it would still not be enough.

They could have a career that pays well and receive many accolades, but still not have any fulfillment. True contentment can only be found in God. Although the woman said she did not have a need or want, once Elisha dug a little deeper, he found out that she did not have a child and her circumstances would not likely permit her to have one. It is interesting to me that Gehazi, Elisha's servant, had to be the one to voice her desire.

I imagine that Gehazi, seeing that her husband was old, thought the woman needed a son who would grow up and take care of her, as was custom, once the inevitable happened and she became a widow. When Elisha delivered the word that she would deliver a child, her reaction revealed that it obviously was a secret desire of hers. I wonder how many well-to-do women are pretending that all is well when they secretly have a longing for what seems unattainable. Whether it be a husband, a child, or a dream business, it is possible with God.

Dreams require certain environments in order to thrive. Faith and prayer are a necessity when one is trying to see a vision come to pass. Doubt cannot coexist with faith. Early on in our marriage, my husband and I had several desires that we knew were to be birthed by God. One was a particular career that my husband was pursuing, and the other was for us to have a child. He was a contract worker for the company in a different position from the one for which we were praying for him to receive. After his contract had ended, we would pray and confess that the position was his. There wasn't an opening at the time, but we did not give up hope. He began to work several different jobs that he hated.

I can still remember seeing him going to work, and each day he looked drained and out of place. He would take off early and even call in some days, and that was not like him at all. Finally, I had a conversation with God and confirmed with Him what I was feeling in my heart.

I poured out my heart to God on my husband's behalf concerning his purpose, and why I felt that it did not benefit our family for him to work for his current employer. All the while, we both were still confessing and believing that the other company would call him back with a permanent position in the department he wanted to work.

The problem was not that he was not successful at his present job. In fact, he was approached about pursuing a career path in management, but we knew that was not God's will. While we were waiting on the promise from God, my husband took some drastic measures. He began to go and sit in the parking lot of the "dream job" and pray and confess that the job was his. When people would ask where he worked, he would state the company's name. I began to do the same. We were not lying because he was still employed as a contractor to work on special assignments. But in our hearts and our confessions, we were not proclaiming a contract position; we were claiming permanency.

Soon after, he was called back to the dream company for another short-term job, and then a position for the dream career became available. There was a test that he was required to pass before he could even be considered for the position. He passed the test but was still not sure if he would get the position.

He decided to step out on faith, so he did not return to the unfulfilling job. It took a great amount of faith to make that decision because it would mean that we would live on one income—mine.

I know some women would not agree with that decision to carry the family financially when their spouse had a job that they quit just because it did not feel like a "purpose job." Most people would say that you work the job you currently have until you get the dream job. In most cases, I would agree, but this was a supernatural situation. When you are expecting something miraculous, you have to step outside of the norm.

It was even bigger than him getting the job he wanted. The bigger issue for me was that when he was in an unfulfilling job that distracted him from his spiritual purpose. When I met him, he constantly talked about what God called him to do. He was passionate about ministering the gospel. Now his conversation was mostly concerning providing for our family. I appreciated his insight to realize that his family was his first ministry, yet I felt compelled to pray through his purpose because I knew that purpose would bring our family to the promises of God.

Praise God! That is exactly what happened next. He received the job and started on the career path that he desired. When you sacrifice for God, He will not only return what you surrendered, but He will also give an increase. Within his first two years, he was offered several promotions and received bonuses and recognition. Then we received the news that we were pregnant. Talk about exceedingly abundant blessings!

Our faith went to an entirely different level! And that was a good thing because we had a fight ahead of us. In the text, the Shunammite woman made a statement that did not align with her current situation. When she was greeted by Gehazi and asked if she, her husband, and her child were okay, she said, "Everything is alright." At the time she made that statement, her son was dead. I have to rewind to the portion of the story when her son died, and her reaction was to lay him on Elisha's bed and shut the door on her way out.

When her husband challenged her to act when the conditions were not right, she gave him the same answer: "It's alright." I get excited when I think about her outlook. Women, we have here an example of a woman of faith. She lay down her issue before God and just trusted that it would be handled. This is the approach we have to take with our concerns. We sometimes have to have an answer, even for our husbands. Even though they are the head, in some instances, they will need encouragement. They sometimes need us to tell them that everything is alright. It is important to know when to stand in that role, and it is when the husband brings the problem *to* us, not when we take it over. When the child became ill, the father sent the child to his mother. He gave the issue over to his wife; she did not take it out of his hands.

The woman was instructed by Elisha to run, stay on course, and not get distracted on her way back to her son. When God gives us instruction, we must be the same way. We cannot try to get everyone else's interpretation of what God wants us to do in our current situation.

What 'Mama and them' instruct us to do may cause us to miss out on God's plan. When I was trying to conceive, everyone had advice on what I should eat, what vitamins I should take, etc. Some people were even bold enough to tell me what sexual position I needed to be in; not only to get pregnant but to determine the baby's sex. Just way too much advice. I had to shut out the voices so I could get instruction from God.

I have some idea of the emotions that could have threatened to take over the Shunem woman because my child's life was threatened in the womb. I will never forget the day my pregnancy took a turn in a different direction—one that could have ended in a miscarriage. I had made it close to five months, and I did not have any issues outside of normal pregnancy conditions. I did not even have one day of morning sickness. I was fairly upset that the experienced mothers had swooped down on me about my heels. I had already planned my maternity experience with fitting dresses to show off my bump and cute pumps to match. So, with humility and what little grace I could scrounge up, I bought some flats.

On the first day I wore flats to work, I had a terrible fall. It was the type of fall that is etched into your memory, and you can replay it exactly as it happened. I remember the moment my foot was caught in the leg of the chair and when I began to fall forward. I didn't just fall; it was almost as if my body involuntarily lunged for the farthest distance from where I tripped. Instinctively, my arm went in front of me to protect my stomach.

I could hear my boss's piercing scream. It all seemed to happen in slow motion like a movie. Lying on the sonogram table, I was very calm. To this very day, my grandmother says she was astonished how calm I was about everything. We were relieved when we found out that the baby was not harmed from the fall, but it was short-lived, as we found out there was another problem. I was diagnosed with an insufficient cervix and would have to be admitted into the hospital to perform a procedure called a cerclage. A cerclage is a cervical stitch that prevents miscarriage or preterm birth. I had never been admitted into a hospital before, and I had never had surgery. I could see a second of fear in my husband's eyes.

Whenever we recant the story, he tells me it does not matter what your faith in God is; when it comes to your wife, there is a split second of fear of losing her when her health is in danger. We prayed, and then we called on our prayer warriors. I sent out a text that said, in essence, "Do not pray and worry because worry breeds fear." Everyone agreed to stand in faith. When my physician came in on the morning of the surgery, she said that she prayed the night before that God would give her the right medical conditions to perform the surgery. That is an amazing feeling, to know that your doctor believes in and relies on the power of God in her practice of medicine. The surgery went as planned, but I was placed on bed rest. From there, a series of complications occurred, including gestational diabetes and fetal growth restriction.

All these labels were placed on my pregnancy and our baby, but we chose not to accept them as a sentence of doom. Instead, we were like the Shunem woman, confessing that everything would be alright. And that is exactly what happened. Our daughter was born small but without complications. She is thriving and growing stronger every day. The Apostle Paul encourages us to be content in every season of our lives. We have to be satisfied in seasons of lack and in seasons of harvest, when we are waiting for the promise and when we receive the promise. We must learn the balance of contentment and pursuit.

Michal:

The One Who Brings Him Down

In the same way, a wife who speaks with God in a way that shows a lack of respect for the authority of her husband, dishonors her husband. Worse she dishonors herself—an ugly sight, like a woman with her head shaved.
1 Corinthians 11:9 (MSG)

Nothing makes me cringe more than to witness a woman cutting her husband down in public. I can only wonder what does she does in private if she conducts herself in that manner in front of others. Titus 2 gives wives instruction to love their husbands and to be reverent in the way they live. For men, love is translated as respect. There are many ways that a woman can show respect, whether it is verbal affirmation, keeping his home, taking care of his children, or meeting his physical needs, just to name a few. All these demonstrations say to that man that as his woman, you give of yourself because of his position in your life.

Understanding the hierarchy of God's kingdom is vital for a successful marriage. The success of marriage is not based on the number of years together or even the couple's measure of happiness. It is measured by how the union brings glory to God.

To bring God glory, the two people must operate in His order—Christ is the head of man, man is the head of Woman, and the head of Christ is God. This scripture reference in I Corinthians 11:3 refers to worship unto God. When we submit to our spouses, we are living a life of reverence unto God according to Ephesians 5:21 where it says, "Submit to one another out of reverence for Christ. Submission is a form of worship." In II Samuel, Chapter 6, David sets out to bring the ark of God to Zion. The ark represented God's covenant with the children of Israel. The lid of the ark, known as the Mercy Seat, was the place where the priest would go to atone for both his sin and the sins of the people.

The term "Mercy Seat" is derived from a Hebrew word *Kapporeth*. *Kapporeth* is thought to have originated from the word *kaphar* which means "cover" or "atone." The same principle of the woman covering her head by submitting to her husband found in Corinthians 11 is the same as God's covering of sin for His people. The husband is the covering for his wife.

After the ark was returned to the city of David, David danced before the Lord, withholding nothing from Him in his praise. From the window, his wife, Michal, watched and despised him in her heart. In our language today, the phrase "look down your nose at someone" would describe Michal's action. She scorned him for dancing in front of the maidens. Several questions come to mind when I read this text. Why was she not praising God with her husband and the rest of the people of Israel?

Why was she so concerned with the slave girls and not the fact that God's presence was now in Zion? We must go back to when we were first introduced to Michal in the book of I Samuel. She was the youngest of King Saul's daughters. When Saul found out that his daughter loved David, he decided to use her as bait. He propositioned David to kill a hundred Philistines in order to marry Michal. Saul believed that David would be killed by the Philistines, but instead, David and his men killed two hundred Philistines. Saul stood true to his word and gave Michal to David as a wife, but that did not stop him from wanting to kill David.

His next attempt was thwarted by his son Jonathan, who was a friend of David. Jonathan warned David, and when Saul tried to kill him by throwing a spear at him, David escaped. Saul sent men to David's house, but this time it was Michal that warned him to flee. She then took an idol and put it in the bed to make it look as if David was in the bed. When her father's men came to kill David, she told them he was lying down sick, but they later found out she was not telling the truth. Saul questioned his daughter as to why she would side with her husband and lie to him. She again lied and told Saul that David threatened to kill her if she did not help him escape.

In either instance, Michal did not have a reason to lie. When the men came to kill David, she did not have to say anything other than he was not there. Her father would not have killed her or held her responsible for David's flight. Even the second lie was unnecessary.

Saul knew that she loved David, so it is likely he would have accepted her assistance to her husband as an act of love. Michal was more concerned with relieving her father's anger than standing by her husband. No doubt that it made Saul more upset with David that he would threaten his child.

Michal's actions to gain her father's approval over the good of her husband and turning her father even more against David with her lies are reflective of toxic issues prevalent in current marriages. Some women are more concerned with the approval of their family and friends than their husbands.

The Bible says that when a man leaves his father and mother, he cleaves to his wife and they become one flesh. When God spoke this assertion over Adam and Eve, they were naked and had no shame concerning their nudity (Genesis 2:24-25). The nudity in the garden represents the exposure we give first to God and then to our spouse. There should be nothing hidden from the two, but certain things should be concealed from everyone else. There should be an understanding established with each of the party's family that they stand with their spouse on all issues that are in line with God's Word. Even issues that are in the gray area should be worked out among the spouses and with godly counsel if needed. The moment you allow mama and them in your relationship because you are mad is the moment you allow confusion into God's already established system: Christ in charge of the husband, and the husband to lead the wife in authority from Christ.

It is important to go to God in those moments when you do not see eye to eye with your partner instead of blabbing to your family. You will eventually get over the issue, but your family may not. Your husband will either feel obligated to do things to get into their good graces or just stay away from your family to keep the peace. His obligation is not to your family, but to you and his children. Pick up any Christian self-help book on marriage, and you are likely to get this advice, but I want to also supply you with a biblical example of how this looks when put into action. Deuteronomy 24:5 (NIV) says:

If a man has recently married,
he must not be sent to war or have any other duty laid on him.
For one year he is to be free to stay at home
and bring happiness to the wife that he married.

This scripture says he is to bring happiness to his wife, not her mama, her daddy, her siblings and so on. That is exactly what it will become: a lifelong mission to please a long list of folks. Who has time for that? Certainly not a man who is focused on God's purpose for his family.

Before my husband proposed, I was offered a job in a neighboring city. It was a job I applied to before I met him and I was torn about whether or not to take it. Eventually, I took the job, and once we were married, he chose to move to where I was located since he traveled for his job anyway. We later found that it was the best decision we could have made.

The first year was a year of major transition and sometimes conflict that brought us closer together. We did not have any family or friends in our business because they were forty-five minutes away. We did not have to explain when we were upset with each other—we just got over it when we got over it. No one knew our issues, which allowed us the room to run to God instead of our comfort zones. I am not saying you have to move where no one knows your name, but you do have to set boundaries for your marriage to work.

As wives, we must stand in righteousness with our spouses. In earlier chapters, I spoke of women who are in the marriage covenant with unsaved spouses, but there are situations where the husband is saved, and his wife has not converted at all or is lukewarm in her faith. Ephesians 5 verse 24, the NIV version states that the wife must submit to the husband in everything. This includes the leading of the family in a life of worship. Of course, the wife has to have a personal relationship with God, but as a family unit, the husband sets the pace for spiritual direction. That husband is still responsible for standing on the Word found in I Corinthians 7:14 that states, "The unbelieving wife is sanctified by her husband." Unfortunately, there is a strong possibility that his spiritual walk will be hindered until his wife comes into total submission to God and to him. It is highly likely that if she is not living a life submitted unto God, it is next to impossible for her to walk in submission to her husband. From her disobedience to God, there is a seed of disobedience in the household that trickles down to the children. The entire household is in a state of confusion.

Before long, the wife will begin to have the same stance as Michal. She will begin to despise her husband. The root issue of David and Michal's marriage was they both had a deceptive nature. It is important not to forget that David deceived Uriah, bore a son by his wife, and ultimately had him killed. It is not surprising that he attracted a liar into his life. We attract what we are. This does not mean we have to be perfect to attract a godly spouse, but it does help to have worked on your issues before you are joined with someone.

The basis of the law of attraction is that if you think or act in a positive manner, you will attract positive people and events into your life. If you live a life of negativity that is what you will attract. The same applies to marriage. You are more than likely to attract a person with the same underlying issues you have but have not dealt with. The problem often occurs when two unsaved people marry, and one spouse receives salvation. That person begins to be delivered but is still faced with who they were before through their unbelieving spouse. Since the lost spouse does not believe in the power of deliverance, they will begin to resent the change in their now sanctified partner.

Be in One Accord

It is evident that Michal did not worship the same God as David because she had idols in her home. The same issue can be the culprit in marriages today. There may not be little statues in the home that one person bows down before or prays to, but if there is anything that is valued more than God, it is an idol.

If what we watch on television, what we wear, or who we associate with takes priority over God and His Word, then congratulations, you have found your idol and the problem in your marriage. Michal could not be excited about the return of God's covering because she was not connected to God. He had no place in her life; therefore, she could not connect with David's act of worship.

If your husband has a relationship with God or even if you believe in God but are not willing to totally surrender as your spouse has, the two of you will not have a connection with each other. You will begin to despise God's place in his life. Amos 3:3 says, "Can two walk together, except they be agreed?" If you two cannot come together in your spiritual walk, there will be no progress in your purpose. You may have individual success, but none that will not be as sweet as the accomplishments that God has awaiting you in the heavenly realm.

The good news is that there is hope for the two of you to be in one accord through the assurance of God's Word. The unsaved spouse has been saved by his or her believing spouse. If you are a woman who is in this place in your marriage where your husband is a believer, and you are not, then this is an opportunity to make a change that will bring peace to your home. You already have a head start because your husband has brought holiness to your marriage. That is what sanctification means—to set apart for special use or purpose; to be holy. The foundation has been established; you only have to walk in it.

You may ask, "What is the first step?" Confession is the first step. Confess to your God that you have disobeyed His order and you need help to make it right. Here is a prayer that you can say aloud to God:

God, I have disobeyed your word which says for me to submit and honor my husband.
I now want to make a change. Help me, Lord.
I confess that I am a sinner and I believe that you died for my sins. Come into my heart and save me. Change me into someone you can use. Be my Lord.

After saying this prayer, go to your husband and humble yourself. Say that you have been wrong and that you want to change. Trust me, the power of God will empower him to forgive and accept you. From this point, God will do something miraculous in your marriage and your home.

Finally, find godly counsel that can help you through the process of transformation. This counsel should be someone who lives by the Word and can give you sound wisdom. Your pastor or even a Christian counselor is a good place to start. Begin to study the Word together and do not be afraid to ask your husband questions when there is something in the scripture that you do not understand.

I know all of this seems easier to read on paper than it is to walk out. The truth is that you cannot afford not to do it. Your family, your children, and your destiny depend on you taking this step. God has so much He wants to do through you and your family, but it must be done in the order of His Word.

The Woman with Issues

For she said, If I may touch but his clothes, I shall be whole.
Mark 5:28 (KJV)

We all at some point in our lives have issues. Issues with our mama and daddy. Issues with our siblings. Issues with our man. The most difficult issues are sometimes those we have with ourselves. *My forehead is too big. I need to lose weight. I wish I were smarter.* Often, we create issues where there are none. As women, we were created to receive and take in. The very fact that we act as receptacles allows us to pull in things that do not belong to us and that we were never meant to carry.

Mark chapter 5 depicts several of the healings Jesus performed. A father pleads with Jesus to come and pray for his daughter, who was dying. While Jesus was on His way to the man's house, many people followed Him, but one woman, in particular, was bold enough to touch Him. She was not touching Him as a spectator or even to be recognized. She had a specific idea, and that was that if she could only touch Him, she would rid herself of the main issue in her life.

The scripture says she had been affected by a bleeding condition for twelve long years. It is amazing how we as women can carry a burden for so long but still be expected to function in life. This woman was said to have spent all she had, but still, she received no results. So many times we search for the answers to our problems everywhere that seems right. After all, who else would she have gone to other than a doctor—the experts on her situation—and yet she still could not be healed. Not only until she went to the source, the creator, was she freed from her past and present pain.

The text does not state the origin of her condition, but it is thought that it was in relation to her menstrual cycle. In those days, a woman with her type of condition was an outcast. Generally, during that time of the month, a woman had to alienate herself until she was no longer menstruating. Since this woman's menstrual cycle was apparently ongoing, she must have been isolated a great deal. How many of us have suffered in isolation and silence? In some cases, you can be around many people but be isolated in your mind, emotions, and even your physical body. When you have pain in your life, there is a tendency to immediately feel as if no one understands what you're feeling. No matter how you try to explain it, people either just do not get it, or they give you their version of, "Get over it." You receive solution after solution, but you feel like you're going deeper in a hole because none of the advice works. I want to encourage you and let you know that there is an answer, and it will work for every situation you may encounter.

Instead of saying there is an answer, I should reiterate: there is someone who is the answer, has the answer, and wants to answer. It does not matter how deep your issue is; God can solve it.

Some of our issues are deep and go way back to childhood. Every time you read the scriptures, there is a new revelation. When researching Mark 5 for the first time, I asked myself why the depiction of the dead girl and the sick woman were connected. I found some connectors in the story that I was able to relate to what God wants to speak to us about in our present-day journey of transitioning.

Grown Women with Little Girl Problems

The first connector I saw was how the text went from the issue of the little girl to the woman's conflict and then back to the dying girl. The text begins with the rich ruler pleading for his daughter's life. Our first issues in life are the burdens of our parents. Because we are all born into sin, we come here with tendencies either brought on by our environments or generational effects passed down to us. Some are born into poverty which breeds issues of self-worth. Others are born with a silver spoon, which opens the door for misplaced expectations of grandeur in life or a complex of whether our identity was earned or given. Then there are those individuals born in destructive families where either drugs, alcohol, sexual immorality or all of the above have ruined generations. Others come from stable families but somehow have found a way to open the door for chaos to reign in their lives. In any of these instances, childhood issues have produced the three-headed monsters that come to wreck our adult lives. They turn strong, accomplished women back to little girls. There is that Mark 5 connector—little girl to woman, and then back to the little girl. Is it not odd that menstruation usually begins during the adolescence stage, but this woman's normal bodily process turned from a coming of age necessity to an adult problem?

In the parallel chapter of Mark 5, we find another of the connectors. Luke chapter 8 verse 42 gives the age of the young daughter of Jairus to be about twelve. The woman with the issue suffered for twelve years with her condition.

The number twelve symbolizes God's power and authority. It is also the number of completion. Jesus Christ was the same age as the dying girl when he began to discuss the law in the temple.

You may ask, "How is all of this connected?" It is likely that if the woman's condition was related to her menstruation, then she was a young girl when she began dealing with her problem. Due to her abnormal cycle, her life would have been full of inconveniences that caused her to be stagnated. Like Jairus' daughter, her situation mimicked death; the death of the freedom that she would experience if she were not plagued by continuous bleeding. In the same manner, when we as women have abnormal circumstances that we are continuously plagued with, we are nursing dead situations. We are like the girl and the woman crying out for someone to come and see about us. Some women's cries are shrill to the ear, while others are muffled pleas that they are too afraid to release.

The connector that breathes life into both of these stories is Jesus. He heard the petition of Jairus for his daughter, and He felt the touch of the sick woman.

In the same way, He still hears the cries of His daughters. Instead of being present to touch us physically, He has given us the authority to live. He is still speaking those words of life to us that He did to the girl in Mark 5: "Talitha Koum" which means, "Little girl, I say to you, get up!" The same authority that Jesus possessed at the age of twelve in the temple, He has given to us.

He is constantly saying to us, "Talitha Koum!" There are so many forces that will keep us bound if we let them. For women, problems in relationships are usually the catalyst to our imprisonment. The sick woman had an "issue" of blood. The word *issue* can be defined several ways, depending on the context. More in line with the sick woman's condition, Merriam-Webster defines the word as "a discharge (as of blood) from the body." It also defines the word as something that people are talking about, thinking about, etc.—an important topic or problem for debate or discussion. I would imagine that it was well known and talked about that the woman was bleeding for twelve years. People love to discuss the problems of the outcast because it makes them feel better about their current state of affairs. I'm sure someone is gossiping about you and what you are going through right at this moment. Or even worse, people are speculating and discussing your past, present, and future.

The bottom line is that you cannot allow the chatter of others to keep you from receiving a touch from God. Your faith is your lifeline, and the moment you let someone poison you with the venom of their words, you are as good as dead, both mentally and spiritually. If Jesus was concerned with what people had to say about Him, we would not have salvation. The people who persecuted Him and tried to defame His name were people who He came to save—His chosen ones. It is the same with us. It can be family, friends, or those we go out of our way to help that will attempt to bring us down. Sometimes it is not their intention to hurt us. Some people just enjoy gossip. Others intentionally set out to hurt you because of jealousy and feelings of low self-worth. No matter the intent, you must rise above it. Separate yourself and live your life according to God's plan.

As a verb, *issue* is defined as a means or place of flowing out. Women in transition are always giving out but are rarely being poured back into. We wear many titles: daughter, sister, wife, mother, friend, working woman, homemaker. Sometimes, we simultaneously operate in them all. The pressure of that, at times, can be daunting. I can remember days as a new mother where I would be up all night with my infant, have to get up early to take my daughter to school, come home clean and cook, and then minister to my husband's needs at bedtime. Any time that I tried to go over my to-do list in my head, I would become exhausted. I had to develop a different plan of attack.

The first thing I penciled in on my list was designated "me time." Whether it is just taking a trip to the store alone or closing the door to the bedroom to nap, I have to set aside some time to just be. My favorite is getting together with girlfriends and catching up on their lives. On our Tuesday night dinners, we walk out the door with the wait staff at closing because we have so much to discuss.
It takes us weeks to coordinate our schedules to get one on the calendar, but we are so refreshed at the end of them. Iron sharpens iron. One of my best friends lives out of town, and we do not talk every day, but when we get on the phone, we are on there for hours. We share recipes, talk about how we have grown as women, and our hopes for the future. We were childhood friends and then roommates.

It is so funny to think that when we were roommates, we would admire the life of the soccer moms. You know them. They are out early in the morning in their white SUVs (I am sure moms drive other colored cars, but they always seemed to be white trucks when we would spot them) with their snazzy sunshades and their cute workout clothes. We imagined that they had just dropped their children off at school and were on their way to the gym, and on from there to leisurely shopping. I now know that waking up super early is not at all glamorous because there is not a promise that you will make it back to your warm bed. I also have a suspicion that they are covering their eyes with designer shades because they have puffy eyes from staying up rocking babies, finishing school projects with children—who told them they had a project at the last minute—and then performing wifely nighttime duties once the children are put to bed. Leisurely shopping is really combing the aisles for the best deals while matching up coupons to save a buck.

Married women are not the only ones who have to learn the meaning of balance. As a young single woman with no children, I was the go-to girl. Family came to me for money, babysitting, and running errands. People automatically think that you have time, energy, and "extra" money to give because supposedly you have no responsibility outside of yourself. At the time, I was glad to do it, because serving kept me from being lonely. I would loan money to family with no expectation of it being returned because I felt good in saying, "I am the lender, not the borrower."

This very day I have family that tells me they would only borrow from me because I did not berate them to pay it back. I learned a valuable lesson from my grandfather to never lend more than you could afford to let someone keep. After a while, I had to learn not to take on other people's problems every time they called upon me. You cannot be a god to people. In some cases, you are hindering their dependence on God by saving them. There has to be a balance and leading from the Holy Spirit in every decision, even in serving others. Otherwise, you will begin to despise your season as a single woman because you will feel used and lonely. This is how many women fall into the trap of coveting a husband—or worse, another woman's husband. With everyone calling on you to be their Superwoman, you will want a Superman to save you. Marriage should be a desire to imitate God, not an escape route from a miserable existence in singleness.

After my divorce, I really valued being single. There is something about being unappreciated as a wife that will make you cherish your freedom as a single gal. When you cook for yourself, you do not have the worry whether it will be enjoyed or picked over. Better yet, you can eat a bowl of cereal and be content if you do not want to cook. As a single woman, you do not have to confer with anyone about where you go, what you do or how you do it. You can just get up and go and do as you please according to the will of God. More importantly, you can serve God in freedom. I Corinthians 7:34 the NIV Version says:

An unmarried woman or virgin is concerned about the Lord's affairs;
Her aim is to be devoted to the Lord in both body and spirit.
But a married woman is concerned about the affairs of this world—
how she can please her husband.

God's Word is so true and relevant. As a single woman, I was able to serve in so many ministries in my local church. I found not only enjoyment in serving but growth in my spiritual life. My prayer life and devotion to the reading of the scriptures was strengthened without limitations of time. I do not want to convey that single women are slothful and have hours of unused time. Many of you are in school, working several jobs, building businesses, and some of you are single mothers. What I am saying is that you have the opportunity to be subject and submissive to only God in your decision making and allotment of your time. Your devotion to God is undivided.

For the single mothers, your life is somewhat parallel to the life of a married woman. In most cases, you have all of the same responsibilities that I referred to above except wifely duties. "Nighttime duties" are not on your to-do list as a single mom! Your release is in Jesus and not in, as they say, "getting your back cracked!" Because, trust me, if you are having sex outside of marriage, more than just your back will be cracked. Yours and your children's futures will be damaged with possibly years of repair work ahead. You want intimacy, not a chiropractic moment by an amateur.

Save yourself some heartache and get an appointment with a professional chiropractor, book a massage, or a spa day with girlfriends when the pressure gets too heavy. You will avoid the headache and heartache that fornication and adultery brings. God is your husband, and you can depend on Him to help raise your children and provide all your needs. He can handle all your issues.

The ultimate takeaway from the passage of the dead girl and the sick woman is that faith is the key to healing and that we as women should never be afraid to reach out to God to be made whole. From the example of the woman with the issue, we must be real with God and bear all. The scripture says in verse 33:

"Then the woman knowing what had happened to her, came and fell at his feet and, trembling with fear, told him the whole truth."

God already knows our struggles, and yet He wants us to bare ourselves before Him. He wants to see your ugly cry. None of the pretenses and facades we put on in front of people will be able to stand in the presence of the Holy One. The beauty in vulnerability with God is that He accepts us for who we are—scars and all. There is a line in the song *Indescribable* by Laura Story that says, "You know the depths of my heart, and you love me the same." I adore that verse. God knows the worst of my sin, fears, and intent in everything, and He still loves me to pieces. That is encouraging for me in those times when I have issues. Knowing this kind of love helps me to say to myself, "Talitha koum."

Abishag:

The One Who Warms His Bed

So his servants said to him, "Let us look for a young virgin to attend the king and take care of him. She can lie beside him so that our lord the king may keep warm.
1 Kings 1: 2 (NIV)

As always, I am fascinated by the invaluable lessons found in the Bible. The old testament especially reads like an intriguing novel with plot twists, and, sometimes, unbelievable stories that if it were not the Word of God I would think I was reading a work of Jackie Collins. Imagine my surprise when I read in I Kings a story entailing a female bed warmer for King David. Apparently when David became old and could not keep "warm," there was a search throughout Israel to find a beautiful virgin to lie with the king and keep him warm. Abishag, the Shunammite woman, was brought to his bed to lie in his bosom and keep him warm. David, being old, was unable to become aroused enough to have sexual relations with Abishag, so she only took care of David.

As I read this account, I became curious as to who Abishag was as a person and what unfolded for her in other scripture. To my disappointment, there was no background history on her life other than where she came from. The only other times she was mentioned was when she was in the middle of a power struggle between two brothers, but still, there was no mention of who she was as a woman. Since she was from Shunem, I looked to the city's history to grasp the place from which she came and what that might tell about her. Shunem was a small village, and its name means "double resting place." It is mentioned two other times in the Bible, the first being the place where the Philistines stayed when they came against Saul in I Samuel 28.

The second is where Elisha was shown hospitality by the wealthy woman, who is also discussed in this book. There was not much from which I could gather to form an opinion of who this young lady may have been. All I knew was that she was a bed warmer for the king.

This knowledge led me to think of a similar modern day arrangement that many men and women have in relationships. It may be a stretch to call these arrangements relationships. Instead, I should just call it what it is defined as a "cuddle buddy." The Urban Dictionary defines a cuddle buddy as a partner with whom one may cuddle with. Usually, not in a relationship with one another, they only seek the affection in physical contact with another person. For all intents and purposes, these two individuals are supposed to only cuddle, with no strings attached. Sounds like David and Abishag's arrangement—contact with no intimacy. The thing is, this would seem an almost impossible task unless you were as David, old and unable to be aroused. What is even more of an issue from a Christian perspective is how a cuddle buddy is related to you finding a mate of purpose.

I understand that not every individual is on the path to marriage, but I only see two options in the Bible as it relates to male and female relationships. The first one is our relations as brothers and sisters in Christ and co-laborers in the gospel. Secondly, we are to be joined as husband and wife. If one chooses not to be married and remain permanently single, then the first option is their only option.

Women often set themselves up for failure in situations such as these. They may succumb to loneliness and just want some male attention. I remember when, as a single girl, I found myself in this situation. It was several years after my divorce, and I was doing well in my journey of celibacy. I was at a point where I was longing for male companionship. When you are single and want to keep accountability in your life, you find yourself always surrounded by female friends or married couples. I was over it. I ended up meeting a nice guy who I began to communicate with over the phone and through some casual meetings. We had great conversations, but I am not sure either of us felt we were on the path to anything really deep. Still, it was nice to break bread with someone other than a female.

One night, I was over at his place and it began to get late. He asked if I wanted to stay over and sleep in his bed and he would sleep on the couch. I immediately received a check in my spirit, but I ignored it. I rationalized that it was late, and he had never shown me he was anything but a gentleman, so I decided to stay. He did as he said and remained on the couch, and the next morning, I went home. Honestly, it felt good to wake up and have a conversation with a man, almost like being married. This feeling of euphoria got me to thinking about what it would be like if we were married. It's funny how I forgot that before that, neither of us felt that the relationship was advancing to anything serious, but after spending the night, I start fantasizing about the "what ifs."

Naturally, this euphoria led me to another night at his house, but this time, he did not sleep on the couch. We decided to have a "cuddle buddy" moment. I am almost positive that this was before the term was even coined. Cuddling turned into kissing, and before I knew it, I was at the "Run, Joseph, Run!" moment. You know the story of Joseph, where Potiphar's wife tried to proposition him, and he had to run out of his coat to get away. That is where I was. Thankfully I was strong enough to stop what was happening, and he was gentleman enough to respect my "no." I explained my position on saving myself for marriage (which I should have done from the beginning), and he respected my decision. The scary thing, looking back, is that the situation could have gone in a whole different direction. It also let me know that I had more work to do when it came to my journey of singleness before marriage. If I was so quick to compromise with the wrong guy, I would go all the way when it came to someone I did consider marriage material.

I know there are some people who do not agree with my position that you should not have a cuddle buddy. My question to them would be, "How does this person fit into your destiny?" I have learned that if a person is not someone God has sent to help push me to my expected end, then I must cut them from my life. There is no time to waste with idle relationships and arrangements. I believe, in many of cases, that there are mixed signals given by both the men and the women. The man is saying he just wants to cuddle when he really wants sex. The woman is saying she just want to cuddle when what she really wants is a relationship.

God created us for relationships. First, He created Adam to be in a relationship with Him. Then, He said it was not good for Adam to be alone, so He created Eve. Man and woman were in a covenant with God and each other. There were no casual arrangements in God's plan, only purposeful connections. If we are to follow the plan of God for our life, then we must not adopt the ways of the world.

As we learn who we are as kingdom women, we will no longer want to compromise in any area of our life. In order to receive God's best, we must live in righteousness. There will always be situations that come to test our standards. In reflecting on the story of Abishag, I wonder how she must have felt when she was sought out for the job to arouse the king. Was she even told that was her purpose? I understand that the times were different, and it may have been an honor to serve in that capacity. There remains the truth that this is all she is known for in history. There is no mention of her accomplishments. As a matter of fact, there is only reference to her failure to do what she was brought in for. We know where she came from and, true to the character of her native land, she was a resting place for David.

Shunem must have been a hospitable city, for the Shunnamite woman that housed Elisha was also known for her hospitality. Women are naturally congenial beings. This is why we were needed in the garden. God told man to subdue the earth. He wanted them to make it a home where they could bask in peace. Women are a great resource in establishing harmony in a dwelling place.

The problem is that, in some instances, we try to establish a home where we have not been invited to dwell permanently. When we are too accommodating to the wrong man, the end results are heartache and anonymity. No one will ever know your accomplishments because you are, like the furniture, a replaceable fixture. The furniture, when new, is held up as a prize to show off, but once it becomes worn, is easily discarded.

A husband is different from a buddy. He will cherish you as his resting place and value you as an asset and not as a superfluous or dispensable commodity. He will want everyone to know not only who you are, but what you have done in his life to make him a better man. A kingdom woman will only commit in a covenant, not a settlement. Abishag was called to David when his old age would no longer allow him to produce. Then she became a pawn in the politics of his sons for the throne. When we get involved in relationships such as "cuddle buddies," we waste time and energy on something that is not productive. A man wants to be joined for life with someone with whom he can build a legacy. Let us wait for the king that will proudly display our name beside his in history books rather than the one he calls when his frailty will allow for him to seek only comfort.

The Woman Who Has Become Too Comfortable

You women who are so complacent, rise up and listen to me; you daughters who feel secure, hear what I have to say! You women who are so complacent, rise up and listen to me; you daughters who feel secure, hear what I have to say!
Isaiah 32:9 (NIV)

We live in a world where complacency is a danger. Many people think more highly of themselves than they ought. Instead of focusing on community, we have become a society that is only concerned with our own personal issues and agendas. Unfortunately, the Christian community has not completely escaped this way of thinking. Although some churches profess to have concern for their neighborhoods and spheres of influence, they are often only concerned with building their church's reputation. Moments of reaching out to the poor become media opportunities. Many want to say, "We have the biggest and the best programs, and oh, yeah, we also help out the little people." This air of superiority has caused the masses to look down on and discount the work of those with sincere agendas.

The Bible is true in that there is nothing new under the sun. The same attitude of laziness toward community was displayed in biblical times. The prophets of old were constantly relaying God's message to forget the self and reach out to those in need. Much like today, people ignored those pleas. As a result, what was considered an outside condition of society became an inward struggle in their own lives. You will reap the harvest of the seeds you plant in other people's lives. That is a principle of God's word.

I remember one of my husband's sermons where he gave an analogy of multiplication to show the threat of only thinking of oneself. He asked the congregation a multiplication fact: "What is five multiplied by one?" They answered, "Five." He continued to ask several facts, all numbers multiplied by one.
He caused a jovial stir when he asked, "What is 23456.333 multiplied by 1?" Of course, no one could remember a number like that for the answer, but the point was that no matter how big the number was,

whenever multiplied by one, it never increased. To increase in our lives, we must empty out to others. This was the appeal Isaiah made to the women of Jerusalem, several times. Isaiah chapter 3:1-7 in the Message Version reads as if it refers to the issues in today's society. It discusses how God stripped Jerusalem and Judah down to bare necessities:

> *The Master, God-of-the-Angel-Armies,*
> *is emptying Jerusalem and Judah*
> *Of all the basic necessities,*
> *plain bread and water to begin with.*
> *He's withdrawing police and protection,*
> *judges and courts,*
> *pastors and teachers,*
> *captains and generals,*
> *doctors and nurses,*
> *and, yes, even the repairmen and jacks-of-all-trades.*
> *He says, "I'll put little kids in charge of the city.*
> *Schoolboys and schoolgirls will order everyone around.*
> *People will be at each other's throats,*
> *stabbing one another in the back:*
> *Neighbor against neighbor, young against old,*
> *the no-account against the well-respected.*
> *One brother will grab another and say,*
> *'You look like you've got a head on your shoulders.*
> *Do something!*
> *Get us out of this mess.'*
> *And he'll say, 'Me? Not me! I don't have a clue.*
> *Don't put me in charge of anything.'*

This text is an accurate description of not only the state of Jerusalem but even the current state of our nation. Due to the rise of evil, there is no longer a sense of being your brother's or sister's keeper. Now, it is every man for himself. Even the withdrawal of authority can be recognized in today's society. Police are tired of being accused of police brutality and, therefore, some choose not to serve and protect. They do so to avoid possible public scrutiny of how they perform their jobs. Parents are afraid of their children. Most people turn away from the responsibility that may put them in the hot seat of public opinion. Granted, there are some voices that are crying out to God for change. I believe that, due to their prayers, God is showing mercy on our land. Unfortunately, the cries of those who are seeking healing for the world are often drowned by the noises of a corrupted culture.

Just as God asked, in Isaiah 6:8, "Who will go for us?" He is still asking the same question. In Isaiah 32:9-20, God made this petition to the women of Jerusalem to forget about their distractions and cry out to God. If you have never read this text, you need to stop right now and read it. I believe when we as women began to use our influence in prayer, we will see a change in the world. Remember earlier in the book, when I said Eve had major influence? So do you, Woman of God.

Now that you have read Isaiah chapter 32, you see that God is calling for us to stand up, but first, we must listen for His instructions. God will only advise us when we have developed a continuous prayer life.

God will not force His will on us, but He will speak to us continuously if we take the time to listen. Think about your first love relationship when you and that significant other would talk on the phone for hours. Neither of you wanted to hang up. That is the type of fellowship that God wants with you. He wants you to long for Him as He does for you. As you establish your "love hour" or hours with God, you will begin to develop a sharp ear to hear when He is giving you direction and warning. This is what He was bringing through the prophet Isaiah to the women of Jerusalem.

Apparently, the women were haughty and self-indulgent. It is a dangerous thing to become complacent. It breeds idleness and dulls your spiritual tools. It is important to note the difference between complacency and contentment. Contentment is gratitude, while complacency is when one is smug and unaware of danger.

The Isaiah 32 women were ladies of means, with fine clothes and nice homes. They did not have to worry about how their children would eat. Earlier in Isaiah chapter 5, it talks about how they lived in extravagant estates where they threw lavish dinner parties that started early in the morning and carried on late into the night. None of the people living these fancy lives wanted anything to do with righteousness. Though their needs were met, they were not overly concerned with those around them who were doing without; this is the problem God had with them. He was not angered by what they had, but rather how their possessions ruled them.

I wonder, are there any women reading this book whose lives resemble those in Isaiah 32? You may be quick to rule yourself out but take a closer look. Are you more concerned about how you look than what you can do for God's kingdom? Is your closet filled with designer shoes and bags, but you see your neighbor's children dressed in dirty clothes every day at the bus stop? Have you even noticed who your neighbors are? Society is obsessed with material trappings. Shoes with red painted bottoms, bags with designer monograms, and expensive homes and cars are now resumé builders. People are overly concerned with perception.

90 Percent Prayer, 10 Percent Skincare

It is funny to me sometimes how people assume they know your status in life based on what you are wearing or where you live. Someone gave me a knockoff handbag that looked pretty authentic.

People would stop me in the store and ask where I got the bag, and when I told them it was fake, they were surprised. A salesperson catered to me more than usual in one particular store. As I began to talk to her more, I saw how she was focusing on my bag. Eventually, she went on to praise it, and when I told her it was not real, you could see her feelings were hurt. I thought it was quite funny, and so did my husband when I told him about it. I even began to become convicted, asking myself, "Is it wrong to carry a knockoff as a Christian?" Are you stealing from the originators, or just buying luxury at your economic level?

After all, is not imitation the highest form of flattery? I am still working on that answer. Even so, it is amazing to me how a purse or a symbol of wealth can uplift someone in other's eyes. It just goes to show you the value that we place on what or whom the masses have deemed worthy.

Imagine if people came up to you or stared at you for carrying a Bible. Why have we not, as Christians, been able to raise the Word of God as the standard for luxury? It is the only thing that will remain when even heaven and earth pass away. This is the message of the text in Isaiah, for women to focus more on those things that are eternal. We should be more concerned about the jewels in our heavenly crown than those on our fingers. I do not want anyone to mistake this as a campaign against wealth or luxurious living. I want a couple of pairs of the shoes with the red bottom and at least one authentic designer bag myself. What I want more is to remain in right standing with God and to fulfill His vision in the earth. I can do that while standing in a pair of Christian Louboutin heels and holding a Louis Vuitton purse, as long as I do not mind kicking off those heels and dropping that bag to do God's work. There is a line in verse three in the rap song entitled *L.A.D.I.E.S* by the rap artist Flame that has become my mantra. It was performed by a featured artist, Da' T.R.U.T.H. The verse says:

Just think about this
You're real fit in Abercrombie and Fitch
And when you in the mall you thinkin' about how to catch fish
Imagine you in Von Dutch on a date
No lust in the place, dude got a crush cause how you hustle your faith
You ain't tryin' be tuck at the waist
Cause you to spend more time in the presence of God

than adjustin' your face
Listen let me cut to chase
And encourage the beauty of holiness you should just
want to be chased

I spend more time in the presence of God than adjusting my face. I read my Word more than I watch Youtube videos on how to style my clothes or hair. The word *more* implies that I partake in all those activities, just not more than the tenants of my faith. Looking cute has never gotten me over any trials and struggles, but getting down on my knees in prayer has done just that and even more. It kept me sane while going through hard times. I strive to exhibit the beauty of holiness rather than the look of the season. Fashion changes with the trees, but holiness never goes out of style.

The beauty of holiness is a lost resource. Someone may ask, "What is the beauty of holiness?" I, myself, asked that question. First, I searched the internet and found the scripture Psalm 96:9 where it says to worship the Lord in the beauty of holiness. Some versions say "in the splendor of His holiness" which translates to strength and glory.

I then asked God to explain what the term means, and He simply answered, "It is my reflection." I was blown away by this answer. All this time and money is spent on makeup, fake hair, fake breasts, etc. to obtain a flawless reflection when we look in the mirror when all we really have to do is seek God's reflection. It illuminates everyone who sees it.

Have you ever spent hours in the mirror to get the perfect look only to see pictures later and you look a mess? On the flip side, have you ever seen a woman with tousled hair and wrinkled clothes, but she has the most amazing glow? I know of two instances where I have seen this occur: a pregnant woman or a woman who spends tremendous time in prayer. Both examples are of women who are carrying life created by God. God's reflection cannot be described in words, but if I were to come close, it would be synonymous with that glow that comes from being impregnated with life. A pregnant woman's glow comes from the illumination of God's creation in the form of a uterus. A praying woman is impregnated with a spiritual uterus. She is carrying the possibilities of God's will in her spiritual womb. If you want your inward beauty to radiate outward, try this experiment. Spend an hour more a day in prayer and see what happens. You cannot spend time in the presence of God and not be illuminated.

2 Corinthians 3:7 speaks of when Moses came down from the mountain after being in God's presence, and how great the glory was upon his face. He was so illuminated that the people could not even look directly at him.

There is a more detailed account of Moses' experience in the mountain in Exodus 24. The first thing I notice in the text was that, although God told Moses to take others with him to the mountain, only Moses could get close to God. God will hear anyone who prays to Him, but only those who developed an intimate connection with God will be called to the top of the mountain. If we want to go higher in our destiny, we must stay in prayer, which brings me to my second observation: Joshua was with Moses on his journey. The text does not say that Joshua went into the cloud with Moses, but evidently, he was close because in Exodus chapter 32 he came back down the mountain with Moses. In knowing that Joshua became the next leader of the children of Israel, I began to relate the fact that he observed not only the ministry of his spiritual predecessor but also his intimate fellowship with God. Joshua waited while Moses was on the mountain with God for forty days and forty nights.

I believe that just as you can have natural mentors, you should have spiritual prayer mentors. Just associating with a person that talks about prayer constantly will push you to want to pray more. Be careful to choose someone whose life lines up with the Word. A person who really has a consistent prayer life will be recognizable. They will act differently and speak differently. You will just know that something greater than them is in operation in their life.

My prayer life seemed to develop new facets after reading Isaiah 32. Maybe you do not live in a large estate or look down on the poor, but have you become complacent?
It is easy to do that when everything in life seems to be going well. A woman will thrive in an environment where there is security. It does not matter if she has everything she wants at the moment if she has what she thinks she needs to live, in most cases, she is satisfied.

There is something about lack that causes us to work harder, even more so when one has lived a life of poverty and has made a vow to never return to that lifestyle. Many times, this is what drives people to overcompensate in their children's lives. They endured a childhood where they didn't have the things they desired and, in some cases, the necessities of life. Children who are lavished with everything they want usually do not have an awareness of the times. They often do not engage in what is going on around them; they are self-absorbed because they are raised to believe that the world revolves around them. I began to think about the history of the children of Israel. By the time Isaiah was written, they were several generations away from slavery in Egypt. I wonder if the wealthy women of Jerusalem were conditioned by their parents to expect to always live in prosperity and not reflect on the years of slavery. The text implies that the women were not aware of the political times and what was going on around them.

It is important as a woman to be knowledgeable about something more than fashion, make-up, and entertainment news. I became a stay-at-home mom after the birth of my daughter. I was concerned that I would become out of touch and only engage in conversations about Pampers and spit-up.

It was important for me to model a well-rounded person to my daughters. I love education and learning. I enjoy reading biblical commentaries and having in-depth conversations about life, history, and spirituality. As caretakers and working mothers, it is easy to become so aloof to the outside world because we are trying to provide a decent life for our families. We cannot afford this stance.

We have to be aware in order to be prayerful.

Live Aware

In the garden of Eden, Adam and Eve were responsible only for working the garden. They could partake of and enjoy any trees other than the tree of knowledge of good and evil. When the serpent came to Eve, and she took a look at the tree she saw that she would gain wisdom of good and evil, she took the fruit and ate and gave some to her husband. As soon as they ate, their eyes were opened. I love the interpretation in the Message version of the Bible. It says in Genesis 3 verse 7, the Message Version, "Immediately the two of them did see what's really going on."

Do we as women really know what is going on around us? In our children's schools? On our jobs? With our spouses? There is evil in our nation that we must address in prayer. I am baffled when I talk to my teenage daughter and hear some of the things that are going on in schools, especially with the young girls. Today it is okay and sometimes celebrated to have sex with a boy on school grounds!
The girls are labeled as having some type of sexual prowess and are awarded with verbal accolades and self-proclaimed titles. They wear bracelets to inform others of what sexual acts they perform and even their sexual orientation. This can be alarming information, but even more so, it should be information we take to disarm the real enemy: Satan.

Disarm the Enemy

The first step I took in disarming the enemy was to teach my daughter to pray. At first, I started by praying every morning with her on the way to school. I wanted to model how she should pray. Then I decided to start the prayer and have her end it. As the days went by I began to hear her pray more in-depth. Her prayers began to become a model of my prayers. I make it a point to pray the scriptures because those are the only words with power. Next, I began to sow spiritual seeds. I bought a book written by a teenage celebrity who is a Christian, and I let her do my talking for me. In most cases, you will not be the major influence in your children's life. In their minds, you are too dumb to know the answers they think they need.

The second area where I disarmed the enemy was in my marriage. My husband and I made an agreement that in times that we could not come to a place of agreement, we would agree to disagree and pray.
That has worked wonders. We rarely disagree now. What happened is that instead of God changing the other person, He gave us an inside view of how to deal with the opposite spouse.
Through prayer, I was enlightened as to what motivates and intimidates my husband. With this knowledge, I now know when I need to keep talking and when I need to just leave it alone.

The third area in which I began to disarm the adversary was in my prayers for other people. The women in Isaiah 32 represented not only the female race but were also a symbol of the cities of Judea. For the purposes of this book, I want to deal strictly with women. The prophet told the women to strip down their expensive clothes and put on *funeral clothes*. In biblical times, to tear one's clothes was a public expression of mourning or grief. Other people would stand at attention at this action. Tradition says if a person tears the clothes over the heart then that is a sign of a broken heart. Does the evil in the land break your heart to the point that you cry out to God to heal the land? Do you pray for those in your sphere of influence who are living in sin? Or are you only concerned with, as they say, your four and no more?

I had to do a self-check as well. I must warn you that after I had carried these scriptures in my heart, I began to lose sleep. God started to wake me at odd hours in the morning to pray for people. Sometimes I knew who I was praying for and other times I did not. I began to notice that the more I prayed for others, the more sharply I began to receive warnings about my own family. I could see danger before it even got close to my door. There goes that principle of multiplication. When you sow into others, you receive more. More prayer equals more power.

When you pray for the safety of the neighborhood and other people's children, you will not have to worry about whether or not your child is safe. They will be covered by default. You will be able to live, as Isaiah 32 verse 18 the NIV Version says, "in peaceful dwelling places and secure homes."

You cannot guarantee peace in your home and community if you are too distracted with self-achievement. Only what you do through and for Christ will last. When we rely on our strength, we eliminate God's power from working in our lives. Isaiah 4 again speaks to the condition of women who are out of touch with God, and the need to depend solely on Him. The chapter can take on both a literal and figurative meaning. In the literal sense, it speaks of how, when trouble came to Zion, the women began to try and secure their own futures.

It was fascinating to see the mentality of modern times in the Bible. Isaiah 4:1 reads:

That will be the day when seven women will gang up on one man, saying, "We'll take care of ourselves, get our own food and clothes. Just give us a child. Make us pregnant, so we'll have something to live for!"

Is this not the same mindset of today's *independent woman*? She does not need a man to take care of her; she just needs him to have a child and for companionship.
This is totally contrary to God's blueprint. In His design, one man and one woman are equal partners, working toward the common goal to build God's kingdom. In this text, there are seven women to one man.

I hate to admit that this happens today as well. Women are fighting over one man, all trying to outdo the other to win the prize. For some, they are not fighting with the other women, but instead are happy that someone else occupies the time with him that they are not willing to give. I wonder what becomes of the children who are a product of this dysfunctional setup. I really do not have to wonder, because the Bible has a few examples of how it plays out. Abraham, Sarah, and Hagar. Jacob, Rachel, and Leah. All examples of women trying to orchestrate their own lives and ending up with an episode of *Sister Wives*. There was no peace in their homes, just self-inflicted chaos.

Some women's homes today look exactly like this. Rather than solely depend on God to build a family, they try and build their own. The result is Baby Mama Drama, child support disputes, and in some cases neglected children. In the figurative sense of this text, God was showing how the women who had become so desperate to seek after their own happiness were a symbol of how His people do the same. The children of Israel and we as Christians try to create our own happiness rather than look to God for instruction. The amazing outcome is that, because God knows that we will mess it up, He created a solution.

In verse 2, it says, "In that day the Branch of the Lord will be beautiful and glorious." That branch is Jesus Christ. He is the answer to our desperation. This is what I love about God. When we forsake Him, and try to do things in our own power, He still has mercy on us and rescues us. Even God's judgment is beneficial. I love how this chapter ends. God cleanses the city with a firestorm and then restores it with His presence. His protection becomes a shade from the heat. In the same way, we create scenarios in our life that bring about the heat of trials. But once we go through the fire, God restores us, and then He covers us as long as we choose to stay in His shade.

I hope that every woman realizes the power she possesses in prayer. Prayer does not require a certain technique, but it does require strategy. The strategy is to pray without ceasing and to pray God's word. Then He will begin to make our way prosperous, and we will have good success as the Bible tells us in Joshua 1:8. We all have had times in our life where we were too preoccupied with life to recognize that we are fighting against ourselves until the moment we surrender to God's way of doing things. We can end the fight and begin to walk in the ease of God's promises. Life in Christ is easy. Sure, we will go through trials and tests. Yes, we will be persecuted. However, we need to take on the attitude of the early church—we need to focus on eternal life with Christ.

This is what drove them to stand for Christ in the face of death. The thing is that right now, in our country, what we call persecution is a mockery of what real martyrs go through.

I am okay if someone laughs at how I live for Christ. At least they are not burning me at the stake. The thing to remember is that unless we begin to pray for our nation, we will have the threat of death for living for God. Everything we hold sacred in our faith is under attack, and the attacks will only get more and more extreme unless we begin to cry out to God.

This appeal is not a call to neglect your family or even yourself. It is important to be a good steward over what and who God has planted in your life. It is equally important to be concerned with what God is concerned with, and that is for His kingdom to come and His will to be done on earth.

Prayer Warrior

*This is the confidence we have in approaching God:
that if we ask anything according to his will, he hears us.
I John 5:14 NIV*

A warrior can be defined as someone experienced in fighting. A warrior does not fight for only the spoils of war, but also for the protection of his territory, the territory of others, or for territory that he wants to conquer. Throughout this book, we have talked about the power of prayer. What I want to explore in this last chapter is your ability as a prayer warrior. Notice I did not say your ability to *become* a prayer warrior. You already are, because you are created in the image of God. God is a righteous warrior, therefore, you are a warrior. You may ask, "How does being a warrior translate in my prayer life?" We can find the answer by looking at this scripture in the Bible that describes God as a warrior. Isaiah 42:13 says in the Message Bible:

"God steps out like he means business. You can see he's primed for action.
He shouts, announcing his arrival; he takes charge and his enemies fall into line.

This should be our stance in prayer. We have to be intentional in our prayers. Our prayers should make the enemy fall in line. The Word already tells us that Satan is fraudulent, yet we seem to fear that he can somehow have power over us. He holds no authority over the saint's life. He has to get permission from God to even cross over into our territory. There have been many times when the enemy has tried to come into my jurisdiction to steal, kill, or destroy. Through the power of prayer, I was able to keep what belongs to me. Earlier on in the book, I talked about the scare I had in my second trimester after a fall. Satan had tried to steal our seed before that incident.

When my husband and I were first married, I wanted to take some time to just enjoy each other, but he was ready to start a family right away. After about four months, something happened—either my biological clock began to talk to me, or my husband romanced me into getting on the same page as he. We began to try to conceive, but it was not an easy road to travel. I cannot tell you how many pregnancy tests we took, only to have our hopes doused in a matter of three minutes.

One day, as I was standing in the bathroom mirror getting dressed, I had a sharp pain in my breast. When I touched it, I felt what seemed like a golf ball-sized lump. Immediately, I felt a surge of panic. I called my husband and had him touch the lump. There isn't much that causes my husband to react, but his face said it all. This was not my imagination; the lump was there. Since I had an annual checkup in a few days, we decided to just wait until that appointment for me to have my breast checked. Every day leading up to my appointment, I was hoping the lump would disappear, but it was still there.

I had never seen fear in my husband's eyes before, but it was present then. Normally, he would tell me I need to pray and have faith, but he was awfully quiet. I think there is something about the threat of a man's family that causes him to react out of character and either get loud or go mute. We prayed together and separately against cancer. My private prayer was that I would go to my appointment and my doctor would tell me there was nothing to worry about.

Unfortunately, that is not what happened. She sent me to the breast care center to get a mammogram and x-rays. When the results came back, there was definitely something there. My husband and I both knew it was time to stop being afraid and go to war.

Before that day, we had both decided to give conception a rest and enjoy our present blessings. After my discovery of the lump, I started to have pregnancy symptoms, but neither of us could get excited about them. I noticed my neck was darker and I had lost a tremendous amount of weight. Then, the ultimate sign manifested: I was several days late. I told my husband that instead of taking a test, I would just wait and see what would happen. I could not get excited because I felt I needed to focus on my current health status.

Looking back, I realize my faith in prayer was not where it should have been. I should have been focused more on the promise than the problem. Yes, there was a possible problem with my breast health, but there was also a possibility that what I had been praying for for months had happened. If I could go back, I would have taken a pregnancy test at home and relished in the joy that I was carrying a child and just give over the issue with my breast for God to handle.

Some may think that I had every right to be worried, but the truth is, that is not kingdom thinking. In the Kingdom of God, we react to what is not seen. My breast issue was just a distraction from Satan that God allowed so that God could manifest our desire to have a baby without my interference.

God knew if I had missed my period, I would have been overly excited about a baby and trying to orchestrate the entire process in my strength. He cannot get any glory from situations that we believe we have a hand in bringing to pass. The fact of the scripture that all things work together for good was evident in this situation. God would get the glory from what happened next.

After we had received the initial results from my mammogram and x-rays, I had to have further testing and wait a week for a specialist to review the results. I remember sitting in the doctor's office, and my husband said to me, "It would be something if the mass disappeared and you were actually pregnant." When the doctor came in, she brought good news. The mass was there, but it had shrunk significantly, and there was no threat of cancer. There was an instant relief for both my spouse and me. It was as if we shifted immediately to the possibility of the promise. With the impending threat of cancer now gone, our focus shifted to my late menstrual cycle. That is exactly how you feel in the victory of battle.

One minute you are fighting for your life, and the next minute, your mind is on to the engagement to conquer new territory. This is the mind of a warrior. You never lose the taste for battle, because you know that while with every victory there may be casualties, there are also new regions to conquer. I told the doctor that my period was late and she decided to send me to have a pregnancy test. Her next words gave both my husband and I chills.

She said that what was happening just may be "a God thing," and she wanted us to be sure to come back and give her the news if I was pregnant. At the time, I wondered how she knew she could say something like that to us. We never once talked about anything personal like faith or our spiritual beliefs. God showed me that a warrior recognizes his cohorts. This doctor obviously was a Christian and her spirit connected with ours.

We went to my doctor's office to take a pregnancy test. The nurses and my doctor's staff were familiar with our story, and how we had been working to have a baby when we ran into a bump in the road. I told the nurse who administered the test about what had occurred with the breast specialist, and I think even she was holding her breath while waiting for the results. After a few minutes, I could see this unreadable expression on her face. It looked like a smile, but I was so on edge that I was not sure. She showed me the test, and for the first time, I saw two bold lines. I had to cover my mouth to keep from screaming. I went back in the waiting room and gave my husband the results.

He was in a state of shock. Sometimes the magnitude of victory in Christ will overwhelm you. We went back upstairs to give the specialist the news, and she had a confidence in her eyes that said, "I knew our God could do it." I learned how to wage war in the spirit because of my cancer scare. As the scripture says, I was wrestling against evil powers. I know someone may be asking, "What does that mean?"

In a wrestling match, the opponents are trying to overpower each other. Each opponent has special moves, some that are familiar to the sport and others that are uniquely theirs. It is the same way in the spiritual battle of prayer. Satan has the same moves that he manipulates to look different in whatever situation a person is facing. Some common tactics he uses are rejection, fear, death, and lies. In my case, he tried to convince me that I would die. As Satan tried to pin me down on the mat with that lie, I would have to overpower him with the scriptures.

In spiritual warfare, the struggle goes on until the stronger opponent gets his competitor to surrender. The thing is, we must train ahead of time for the fight. If I did not already know that the Word says that Christ was "wounded for my transgressions and bruised for my iniquity" and other healing scriptures, I would have been defeated. One must have the proper armor in order to be successful in battle. This is what distinguishes a warrior from a fighter. In biblical warfare, the warrior's armor was customized because he faced the threat of danger more than just a normal soldier. He was always the target. The same rules apply in spiritual battle. The stronger you are in prayer, the more intense the attacks will be.

Do not get confused and think that this means that the enemy will not attempt to attack you if your prayer life is not top level. The scripture says that the adversary prowls around seeking whomever he may devour. This means he is attacking everyone.

He will devour the weak first because they have nothing with which to fight, and he will send the heavy arsenal for those who can go toe-to-toe with his forces in battle. Your armor is the Word of God and the spiritual tools found in His Word. This is the only way to win against Satan. You have to constantly remind him of your future, and *his* future due to his disobedience.

In spiritual war, God will send you reminders that you are never fighting alone. It may be the little old lady at your church, who always encourages you to never give up and shares how God was there for her and her family. It may be some stranger you encounter, who tells you about how they overcame their issues that seem exactly like what you are currently facing. Though we as Christians face different battles, we all are fighting the same forces who have already been defeated. Imagine if it was being publicized that the two best boxers in history were going to fight, but the match was fixed for one of them to win. Would most people even pay HBO money to order the fight, already knowing the results? Curiosity may get the best of some people, but most people would just wait for the major clips to be broadcasted on Sports Center.

This is the attitude we should take as Christians. Jesus already won the victory for us and determined Satan's future, so why are we so overwhelmed in the fight when we know the results? We should go into the fight knowing our opponent's every move and taunting the enemy with the fact that we already have the victory.

As I move higher in my faith, I still fight the enemy as hard as I can, but I have a different perspective. I am not worried about if I will win, but instead, I think, *how* am I going to win? I ask God questions such as, "How much ground are you going to let Satan get before you come in and knock him to his knees?" See, I understand that sometimes I will lose people and things, even those that I hold dear. Even in that, I have confidence and know that whatever I lose, something better is on the other side of triumph. Now it is time for us to get specific about how we fight. 2 Corinthians says:

"For the weapons of our warfare are not carnal,
but mighty through God to the pulling down of strongholds."

This means you cannot fight the adversary with a bat. In natural fighting, any time you use a weapon, there is a possibility that the other person could take your weapon and use it against you. Not so in spiritual battle. The devil has no desire or authority to use our weapons, and his weapons are powerless against the power of God's word. We also have accompanying weapons to the Word. Ephesians 13-18 in the Message Bible sums it up best:

Be prepared. You're up against far more than you can handle
on your own. Take all the help you can get, every weapon God
has issued, s that when it's all over but the shouting you'll still
be on your feet. Truth, righteousness, peace, faith, and salva-
tion are more than words. Learn how to apply them. You'll
need them throughout your life. God's Word is an indispen-
sable weapon. In the same way, prayer is essential in this
ongoing warfare. Pray hard and long. Pray for your brothers

and sisters. Keep your eyes open. Keep each other's spirits up so that no one falls behind or drops out.

Truth, righteousness, peace, faith, and salvation are the tools we use against the enemy. Once we are armed, there is a daily battle that takes place where we must wage war to keep the enemy's lies from infiltrating our camp. I say camp because we are not in war alone. We are a body of believers fighting against spiritual wickedness in high places. This is why the scripture says, "Keep each other's spirits up so that no one falls behind or drops out." We have to develop buddy systems in the kingdom. A buddy system is defined as "a cooperative arrangement whereby individuals are paired or teamed up and assume responsibility for one another's instruction, productivity, welfare, or safety." There is strength in numbers. We should make it our business to wage war for other believers in prayer. God often wakes me up at night to pray for people. I know others are praying for me. I rejoice in the productivity of the saints. Ground gained by another Christian gives me access to that territory. We also have to wage war for those falling behind or who drop out. Christ sent the disciples out two by two.

My husband is a military man, and he often talks about the system of having a "battle buddy." Each soldier is assigned to a partner that they have to assist when they are in and out of combat. One of the reasons this system was established is to keep down the rate of suicide in the military.

Battle weighs on you if you allow negativity and the fatality of war to overtake your thoughts. Spiritual war can have the same results. You have to stand in the hope of God's Word and not let negativity in your mind. You cannot allow yourself or your battle buddies to self-destruct. Satan is counting on the lies he tells you to convince you to give up. Do not let him win. Stand up and fight. Arm yourself with truth. Know that you already have the victory.

We have to be honest with God in prayer like the biblical heroine, Hannah, when she petitioned God for a child. In 1 Samuel chapter 1, we see that Hannah was almost at the point of desperation. She was constantly crying, and at one point, she did not eat. The scripture says that Hannah stood up and cried out to God. Even though she was in a state of bitterness, she knew the One who had the power to change her situation. She wept, and she prayed. She prayed, and she wept. She was naked before the Lord in her emotions. She prayed in a manner and for so long that Eli, the priest, thought she was drunk. We have to continue to petition the father even when others do not understand or know what we are doing.

People will question why you are praying for the same thing for years, or ask you why you have not given up on that prayer request. You have to keep praying and believing that what you prayed for will come to pass. And it will. Hannah believed, and God blessed her with a son, Samuel. I love what happens at Samuel's dedication.

Hannah reminded Eli that she was the same woman who was standing in that same spot not long ago, praying for a son and that she was now standing with him and dedicating Samuel to God. Then, Eli worshiped God with Hannah. Even the one who thought she was drunk when she was praying had to recognize what God did for her. The same goes for you. When God answers your prayers, everyone who thought you were crazy will have to recognize the power of prayer. Someone may be asking, "How do I even develop a prayer life?" First, we must eliminate the myth that prayer has to be difficult. Jesus gave us a model in Matthew 6:8-13:

Therefore do not be like them. For your Father knows the things you have need of before you ask Him. In this manner, therefore, pray:
Our Father in heaven,
Hallowed be Your name.
Your kingdom come.
Your will be done
On earth, as it is in heaven.
Give us this day our daily bread.
And forgive us our debts,
As we forgive our debtors.
And do not lead us into temptation,
But deliver us from the evil one.
For Yours is the kingdom and the power and the glory forever. Amen.

Many people learn this prayer as a child. Jesus was not instructing us to pray this exact prayer but to pray in this manner. First, we must acknowledge that God is our Father and that He is in heaven, signifying His sovereignty in our lives. Just think about your relationship with

God and how it correlates to the characteristics of a natural father. God provides what we need when we ask.

He is there for us when we are sad or lonely. He wipes our tears, and He is there to catch us when we fall. He brings correction to our lives when we are wrong, and He loves us through our mistakes. As you meditate on how God is a Father to you just begin to express it to Him in your own words. It does not have to be a ten-page letter unless you desire it to be.

Next, we must hallow the name of God. God has many names that describe His character. He is Jehovah Jireh, our provider. He is Jehovah M'Kadesh, our sanctifier— I could go on and on. When we hallow, or honor, God's name as holy, it reminds us of what He is to us and what He does for us. Also, there is power in knowing who your God is. In prayer, we can identify exactly who we need God to be at that moment. If you are suffering from illness, you can honor God as Jehovah Rapha, your healer. If you need peace, God to you will be Jehovah Shalom and Jehovah Shammah; He will be your peace, and He will be present in that moment. The next portion of the prayer talks about God's kingdom come and His will to be done on earth as it is in heaven.

This is reminding us that God has a plan already mapped out in heaven, and we only need to ask Him to manifest it here on earth. He wants us concerned about His kingdom. The kingdom of God is righteousness, peace, and joy in the Holy Ghost.

When we ask God's kingdom to come, we are attracting righteousness, peace, and joy into our lives. There is a heavenly transference of all that God has stored up for us in heaven. It is like getting a download here on earth.

The next part of the prayer gives us the ability to address our needs.

We ask God to provide our daily bread, which translates into our necessities and the necessary scripture we need to sustain our spirits. One thing I have learned to do is to ask God to give me a word from Him that keeps me strong throughout the day—to be a light in dark places. Then, I give my day over to God. I ask Him to go before me to make every crooked way straight. When I do this in the morning, I have my best days. I remember every task I need to get done. The Holy Spirit is like my secretary when I pray this prayer. The Spirit keeps me on point. Everything I need is available to me.

Next, we must work on our heart. We ask God for forgiveness and to help us to forgive those who have wronged us. I ask God to create in me a clean heart and renew a right spirit within me according to Psalm 51:10. Then, I ask for forgiveness of sins of omission and commission. I ask Him to reveal every hidden sin and cleanse me from it. Then I ask for Him to help me to forgive quickly. *And do not lead us into temptation, but deliver us from the evil one.* This part of the prayer is sometimes misunderstood.

The first thing to address is that God does not bring temptation to us. James 1:13 says:

Let no one say when he is tempted, "I am being tempted by God," for God cannot be tempted with evil, and he himself tempts no one. What this means is that we ask God not to allow us to fall into the temptation of Satan. 1 Corinthians 10:13 tells us that God will not let us be tempted beyond what we can handle. It also says He will provide a way for us to escape temptation. I pray this portion for both myself and my family. I pray that my husband is not tempted at his job, nor my children at school. I cover us all in the blood. The last part of the prayer goes back to us recognizing the sovereignty of God and giving Him glory. We recognize His power in our life. I take the time to remind God of every present blessing He has bestowed upon me.

If you use this format to pray every day, you will begin to develop a prayer life that will become deeper by the day. I also have books that teach me to pray the Word of God. God tells us to put Him in remembrance of His Word so that we can be vindicated in Isaiah 43:26. As you learn more scriptures and apply them in prayer, you will begin to see results in your life. You will begin to develop confidence in the Word and in the fact that God hears your prayers.

Praise and worship are also mighty tools that set the atmosphere for spiritual war. When Jehoshaphat, king of Judah, was threatened by the Moabite alliances, he asked God to be his vindicator. He ordered a nationwide fast and waited for instruction from God.

God spoke through Jahaziel that He would protect and fight for His people. The next day, Jehoshaphat ordered the praise and worshippers to march ahead of the troops, singing. 2 Chronicles 20 goes on to tell how the Moabite forces began to fight against themselves and the victory was won for Judah. Not only did they win the battle, but they also walked away with equipment, clothing, and other valuables.

War is not always fun, but if you are on the winning team, it is always beneficial. We always win in prayer. It is the most important tool in my Christian walk. It is my lifeline—my connection to the Creator. It is my weapon of choice. I encourage you to never cease praying. Like Hannah, pray even when you are desperate and bitter. God will go before you when you cry out to Him. It says it in His Word in Deuteronomy 31:8. It reads, " The Lord himself goes before you and will be with you; he will never leave you nor forsake you. Do not be afraid; do not be discouraged."

Conclusion

The transitions through womanhood are complex. We are daughters, sisters, wives, and mothers. Our focus has to shift from family, to work, and for some, to ministry—sometimes while balancing all three simultaneously. At some point, we find ourselves struggling to find the answers to obtain the life we always dreamed of having. This is why, in the supermarket, you see magazine covers with headings such as, "How to Balance Motherhood and Career" or "Can Women Really Have It All?"

The answer is yes when we rest in God and His purpose for our lives. In every transitional phase, it is important that we rely fully on God's plan to help us to fulfill our destiny. This book offers an opportunity to identify our womanhood as a calling from God and not a list of tasks.

In my life, I am always searching the Bible for examples of how biblical women navigated the challenges of the female experience. In this book, I hope I offered God-inspired revelations from the stories of the female generals and antagonists. I also wanted to be transparent and share examples from my own life in hopes that you would not feel alone with the issues you face.

I wrote this book because I wanted to prevent my daughters and yours from making some of the same mistakes I made. I wrote it for myself, so I would always have a reminder that God has always own what I would face as a woman because there were others before me who have triumphed over the same obstacles. I pray that we always remember that God's grace is sufficient to carry us through every test and trial.

About the Author

SHAYLA HICKS is a wife and mom whose heart has been moved by God to start a movement where women rely on the Word of God rather than cultural pressures as they navigate through their journey of salvation. She counsels women to trust God not only with their lives but to seek Him for their ultimate purpose. Shayla and her husband Richard live in Vicksburg, MS and are the founders of Partners in Christ Ministry.

How to Contact

Email: shaywynn1@gmail.com

Instagram: www.instagram.com/mrs_hicks_i_am/

Facebook: www.facebook.com/shayla.wynn.9

www.facebook.com/Iamintransition/

Blogspot: www.shaylahicks.com

www.ingramcontent.com/pod-product-compliance
Lightning Source LLC
LaVergne TN
LVHW051606070426
835507LV00021B/2807